PENGUIN BOOKS — GREAT FOOD

The Chef at War

Born in France, ALEXIS SOYER (1810–1858) was a celebrated chef and kitchen innovator. He became the first chef at the Reform Club in London, where he instituted many innovations in the kitchens, including cooking with gas and using refrigerators cooled by cold water and ovens with adjustable temperatures. His kitchens became so famous they were opened for tours, and his 'lamb cutlets Reform' still features on the menu at the club today. Later on in his life, Soyer campaigned for better food, setting up soup kitchens in Ireland during the potato famine and offering his services to British soldiers during the Crimean War, training chefs, organizing provisions and using his own invention, the Soyer stove (a portable stove), in the field to cater for troops. The stove was still in use in the late twentieth century.

The Chef at War

ALEXIS SOYER

PENGUIN BOOKS

PENGUIN BOOKS

Published by the Penguin Group
Penguin Books Ltd, 80 Strand, London WC2R 0RL, England
Penguin Group (USA) Inc., 375 Hudson Street, New York, New York 10014, USA
Penguin Group (Canada), 90 Eglinton Avenue East, Suite 700, Toronto, Ontario,
Canada M4P 2Y3 (a division of Pearson Penguin Canada Inc.)
Penguin Ireland, 25 St Stephen's Green, Dublin 2, Ireland
(a division of Penguin Books Ltd)
Penguin Group (Australia), 250 Camberwell Road,
Camberwell, Victoria 3124, Australia
(a division of Pearson Australia Group Pty Ltd)
Penguin Books India Pvt Ltd, 11 Community Centre,
Panchsheel Park, New Delhi – 110 017, India
Penguin Group (NZ), 67 Apollo Drive, Rosedale, Auckland 0632, New Zealand
(a division of Pearson New Zealand Ltd)
Penguin Books (South Africa) (Pty) Ltd, 24 Sturdee Avenue,
Rosebank, Johannesburg 2196, South Africa

Penguin Books Ltd, Registered Offices: 80 Strand, London WC2R 0RL, England

www.penguin.com

A Culinary Campaign first published 1857
This extract published in Penguin Books 2011
This edition published for The Book People Ltd, 2011
Hall Wood Avenue, Haydock, St Helens, WA11 9UL

1

Set in 10.75/13pt Berkeley Oldstyle Book
Typeset by Jouve (UK), Milton Keynes
Printed in Great Britain by Clays Ltd, St Ives plc

Cover design based on a pattern from a mess plate for the English
navy, *c.* 1840. Blue and white transfer-print on earthenware.
(Photograph copyright © Bridgeman Art Library.) Picture research
by Samantha Johnson. Lettering by Stephen Raw

ISBN 978–0–241–96070–7

www.greenpenguin.co.uk

Contents

How it All Began

'Hurrah! hurrah! bravo! bravo!' For a few minutes rounds of applause and shouts of laughter from the juveniles were heard and loudly re-echoed throughout the vast cupola of Old Drury, sending home the delighted spectators, in fits of sneezing and coughing, through a variegated atmosphere. Sir Henry W—, turning to me, exclaimed, 'Hallo, Mr. Soyer, the pantomime is over early this evening!' and looking at his watch, continued, 'Why, it is only half-past eleven o'clock.'

[. . .]

In a few minutes the theatre was nearly emptied of spectators, but still full of smoke. Considering myself that evening as free as a butterfly on a spring morning, though unable, like that light-hearted insect, to flit from flower to flower, I was trying to escape, with the swiftness of an eel, down the gigantic and crowded staircase, hoping to get off unobserved, as I had to start early in the morning for the country, when suddenly a friendly hand pressed me forcibly by the arm. The owner of the same cried, 'Stop! Stop! my friend; I have been hunting all over the theatre for you.' I at once recognised an old Devonshire acquaintance, whom I was indeed much pleased to see, having received a most kind reception

1

from him at my last visit to that delightful county – so justly named the garden of England.

'Well, my dear sir,' said he, 'myself and several acquaintances of yours are here for a few days, and have ordered a supper this evening at the "Albion." We heard you were at Drury Lane, and I have come to ask you to join us.'

[. . .]

Finding it almost impossible to get out of it, and my friend having promised we should break up early, I accepted, saying, 'You must allow me to go as far as the "Wellington," as I have an appointment there; I will be back in about half-an-hour.'

My incredulous country friend would not grant permission till I had assured him that I would faithfully keep my promise, and return.

[. . .]

We parted, he going to the Albion, and I to the Wellington.

On my arrival there, I found that my friend had been and was gone. My intelligent cabby soon brought me back through the dense atmosphere to that far-famed temple of Comus, at which crowds of celebrities meet nightly – some to restore themselves internally, others to sharpen their wits at that tantalising abode of good cheer. Upon entering, I inquired of a waiter, a stranger to me, if he could inform me where my six friends intended to sup.

'Yes, sir, directly.' Speaking down the trumpet: 'Below! a Welsh rarebit and fresh toast – two kidneys underdone – scalloped oyster – a chop – two taters! Look sharp below!'

To the barmaid: 'Two stouts, miss – one pale – four brandies hot, two without – one whisky – three gin – pint sherry – bottle of port!'

'What an intelligent waiter!' thought I, 'to have so good a memory.' Having waited till he had given his orders, I again said, 'Pray, my fine fellow, in which room are my friends going to sup? They have a private room, no doubt?'

'Yes, sir, a private room for two.'

'No, not for two – for six.'

'Oh! I don't mean that, sir: I want a rump-steak for two,' said he; 'stewed tripe for one – three grogs – bottle pale Bass.' And off he went to the coffee-room.

'Plague upon the fellow!' said I to myself.

As the barmaid could not give me any information upon the subject, and I perceived through a half-opened door on the right-hand side of the bar a table laid for six, I went in, making sure it was for my friends, and that they had not yet arrived. Indeed, I had myself returned from my appointment much sooner than I had expected. I sat down, and was reading the evening paper, when a waiter came in. 'After you with the paper, sir.'

'I have done; you may take it.'

'There's the *Times*, sir, if you have not seen it.'

'No, I have not; let me have a look at it.' After reading one of the leaders, my attention was drawn to a long article written by the Crimean correspondent of that journal. When I had read it carefully a second time, a few minutes' reflection on my part enabled me to collect my ideas, and established in my mind a certain assurance that I could, if allowed by Government, render service in the cooking of the food, the administration of the same, as well as the distribution of the provisions. These were matters in which I could detect, through the description of that eye-witness, the writer of the above-mentioned article, some change was much needed. I therefore wrote the following letter to the *Times*, it being then nearly one o'clock in the morning: –

THE HOSPITAL KITCHENS AT SCUTARI.

To the Editor of the Times

Sir, – *After carefully perusing the letter of your correspondent, dated Scutari, in your impression of Wednesday last, I perceive that, although the kitchen under the superintendence of Miss Nightingale affords so much relief, the system of management at the large one in the Barrack Hospital is far from being perfect. I propose offering my services gratuitously, and proceeding direct to Scutari, at my own personal expense, to regulate that important department, if the Government will honour me with their confidence, and grant me the full power of acting according to my knowledge and experience in such matters. I have the honour to remain, Sir,*

Your obedient servant,

Feb. 2, 1855. A. Soyer.

After despatching this letter, I again inquired about my friends and my anticipated supper, which for some time had escaped my memory. 'Did you ring, sir?'

'No, I did not, sir, but the bell has,' recognising my stupid waiter.

'Oh, sir! are you here?'

'Of course I am; don't you see me?'

'Well, sir, your friends have had supper; they inquired everywhere for you; I told them you could not wait, as you had two ladies to see home as far as Brompton.'

'You foolish fellow! I never spoke to you about ladies, Brompton, or any such thing; I merely asked you where my friends were to sup; to which you replied, "Rump-steak for two, tripe for one, two taters, pat of butter, one pale Bass, and three kidneys for a gentleman, under-done."'

'No more you did, sir. It was number three who told me to say so; not you, sir; you're quite right, sir!'

'I am sure I am right; but as for you, your head is quite wrong!'

'Well, I assure you, sir, we have so much to do at times, we hardly know what we are about.'

'I don't think you do,' said I, sharply.

'But I tell you what, sir, they are there still, and you had better go to them.'

'No, it is too late now; give them this note from me when they go out; and here is sixpence for yourself, for through your mistake you have after all rendered me a service. I did not wish to come here this evening, as I have an early engagement for tomorrow, so I will have a bit of supper and go home.'

'Well, do, sir; I thank you, and am very glad I have given you satisfaction at last.'

'Send Little Ben here; he knows what I like for supper.'

'Hallo, Mr. Soyer, everybody in the coffee-room has been inquiring after you this evening,' said Little Ben upon entering.

'I know; but that foolish waiter who was here just now made such a mull of everything, that he quite upset our party; I could not get any answer from him, so I made sure this table was laid out for us, and here I stuck.'

'No, sir, your friends supped in the coffee-room, and are still there, if you like to have your supper near them.'

'No, no; give me what you like here.'

'What shall it be, sir? – oysters, broiled kidneys, chops, steaks, stewed tripe, broiled bones?'

'Have you nothing else?'

'Yes, sir, grilled fowl and scalloped oysters; only they will take some time preparing.'

'Well, give me scalloped oysters, and my favourite Welsh rarebit, made in my style – you know; a pint of port wine, and fresh toast for the rarebit.'

'Yes, sir; the cook knows – I'll tell him it is for you.'

'But how is it you never vary your supper bill of fare? It is very scanty of choice for such a large tavern as this. I do not mean to complain, but give a little change now and then, by introducing a few new dishes.'

'Ah! you're right, sir; it would please the customers, and be much better for us waiters, to have something new to offer; but, bless you, sir! I have been many years in this place, and it was always the same; and no doubt will remain so for as long again, unless a gentleman like you takes it in hand – they would then attend to it; but, of course, you have something else to do.'

'So I have; yet I don't see why, in my next book upon cookery, I should not devote a few pages to the London suppers. I intend doing so, and, when published, I shall be happy to present you with a copy.'

'That will be first-rate, sir; I thank you, and won't I recommend the new dishes *à la* Soyer, as some of our customers call them!'

'Well, my man, upon second thoughts, as you seem so anxious about it, and I am not going to join my friends, give me a pen and ink, and while supper is preparing, I will write a few practical receipts, which can be easily introduced without interfering with your duty or the kitchen; they will, no doubt, prove agreeable to your customers, who are in general a class of *bon vivants*, fond of good things as well as of variety in the bill of fare.'

'Here is the pen, paper, and ink, sir.'

'Thank you; come again in about twenty minutes, and they shall be ready; or, if you are not in a hurry, stay.'

'No, sir, I am not; our supper business is over.'

'Well, now listen: first, I do not intend to criticise your bill of fare, which is as much varied, if not more so, than that offered at other large taverns, and it is quite as well executed. Now, respecting kidneys – you consume a large quantity of them?'

'So we do, sir.'

'Then I will give you a receipt or two for dressing them: –

No. 1. – Take two kidneys, split them lengthways as close to the sinew as possible without parting them; remove the thin skin, lay them flat upon the table, and season rather highly with salt and pepper; then run them crossways upon a wooden, metal, or silver skewer, forcing the sinew upwards; this will prevent their curling up again while cooking. Next dip them in some well-beaten eggs, to which you have added about a tablespoonful of dissolved butter; or rub them over with a paste-brush, which will do it more equally; roll them in fine breadcrumbs, and slightly beat them on both sides with the flat of your knife to cause the crumbs to stick to the kidneys. Put them upon the gridiron, over a sharp fire, at a proper distance; they will require from five to eight minutes doing, according to size.

For the uninitiated, the following plan is the best to ascertain when they are properly done. Press with the prongs of a fork or the point of the knife upon the thick part of the kidney; if done through, it will feel firm and elastic to the touch. When the kidneys are done, slip them off the skewer on to a hot dish, and place in each a piece of butter, à la maître d'hôtel, about the size of a small walnut; send to table, and by the time it reaches the guest, the butter will be half-melted; quite so when the kidney is cut by the customer, who, by turning the pieces and blending the butter with the gravy, will make a rich sauce, and partake of a delicious as well as a wholesome dish.

'Partaking of overdone kidneys at night is the forerunner of the nightmare.'

'You're right, sir; that it is,' said Little Ben; 'for at times we have some left, and keep them warm for supper; and they get as tough as pieces of leather, when after eating three or four – and I am always very tired at night – I never can sleep. Now I think of it, the tough kidneys must be the cause; and if I do sleep, Mr. Soyer, I have such awful dreams that I feel more fatigued when I rise than when I go to bed.'

'Of course,' I replied, 'I am well aware of that; they cannot digest; therefore, you see the importance of having them properly done.'

'Very much so indeed; I quite understand it now, and perceive that if they cannot at all times be done to perfection, underdone is much preferable to overdone. I perfectly understand you, sir; but you see we require such a quantity.'

'Well, I have only given you the receipt for two. I will now, if you like, give you the receipt for a hundred.'

'Do, sir; that will suit us better.'

'I suppose they are most in request for supper?'

'Indeed they are, sir.'

'Then, in the course of the day, the cook should prepare a hundred precisely as the first – viz., ready for cooking. They should be put upon skewers, two, three, or four in a row; so that, when called for, he has only to remove them from the larder to the gridiron. About two pounds of butter à la maître d'hôtel should be prepared and kept in a cool place to be ready when required. By following this plan, you could easily cook several hundred during the evening, if called for. Should any remain unsold, they will keep till the next day, and will only require rolling in the crumbs again previous to broiling.'

'I see, sir; it will save a great deal of time by having them prepared beforehand.'

'But suppose you had none prepared beforehand, a

dozen can soon be got ready by an active cook. The addition of the dissolved butter to the eggs keeps the kidneys fresh and moist, and inserting them upon the skewer retains them flat, and they are cooked more regularly in half the time, while without the skewer they curl up, and are frequently underdone on one side and cooked too much on the other.'

'I plainly understand what you mean.'

'These details upon the same subject are perhaps tedious to you.'

'Not at all, sir; I see the importance of them.'

'Well, the other receipts will come quite plain and easy to you. To tell the truth, I have had those overdone kidneys upon my conscience for some time. Mind, I do not intend to erase the plain broiled kidneys from the supper bill of fare, for I am very fond of them when properly cooked.'

'They are very good; and many gentlemen will not have them any other way.'

'Well, I do not blame them, for they are both agreeable and nutritious that way; but here is another appetizing receipt, which we will call à la Roberto Diavolo.'

No. 2. – Put two plain kidneys upon a skewer, and with a pastebrush butter them over. Set them upon the gridiron as near the fire as possible, for they cannot be done too fast; turn them every minute, and when half done season with salt, pepper, and a small spoonful of cayenne; chop some gherkins and a little green chillies, if handy; or, instead of either, a tablespoonful of chopped piccalilli with the liquor. Put these on a hot plate, with a teaspoonful of lemon-juice and a pat of butter. Take up the kidneys, and slip them burning hot from the skewer to the plate; turn them round four or five times in the mixture, and serve immediately. A small piece of glaze added to the butter will prove a great addition. Three, four, or five minutes will do them, according to the size.

KIDNEYS À LA BROCHETTE, PARIS FASHION

The Parisian *gourmet* would not eat a kidney if it was not served upon the silver skewer; the only merit of which is, that they keep hot longer and look better than when the skewer is omitted; as they often shrink, especially if the sinew has not been properly divided in the splitting of them.

'As, no doubt, you have something to do, you had better leave me; I will write a few more receipts. Bring me my supper in a quarter of an hour, and they will be ready.'

'Very well, sir; I will give a look round and order your supper.'

To the minute Little Ben walked in with the scalloped oysters, which I must admit looked remarkably tempting. He handed me my supper, but upon reflection I did not hand him the receipts, only a list of their names, intending to put them into the cookery-book I had promised him, knowing well enough that it was not in his power to bring them out. He thanked me for my lecture on cookery, as he called it, and the following bill of fare. I paid my bill, and left.

NEW BILL OF FARE FOR TAVERN SUPPERS

Rump-steak and fried potatoes; ditto with shalot, pimento, and anchovy butter. Relishing-steak, fillet of beef à la Parisienne; ditto à la Chateaubriand.

Mutton chops à la bouchère; ditto semi-provençale; ditto Marseilles fashion; ditto with relishing sauce.

Plain cutlets with fried potatoes, à la maître d'hôtel, à la Sultana, semi-provençale.

Lamb chops à la boulangère, à l'Américaine, à la printanière.

Pork chops with pimento butter, à la Tartare; ditto camp fashion.

Veal cutlets en papillote; with maître d'hôtel butter; with relishing butter; with fried potatoes.

Kidneys on toast, semi-curried; ditto with sherry or port; ditto with champagne. For kidneys à la maître d'hôtel, à la brochette, and à la Roberto Diavolo, see Receipts, pages 7–8, 10–11.

Stewed and curried tripe; ditto Lyonnaise fashion.

Lobsters au gratin in the shell; scalloped ditto; curried on toast; lobster cutlets; new salad, Tartar fashion; plain salad with anchovies; crabs au gratin in the shell; crab salad with eggs.

Grilled chicken and Sultana sauce; à la Roberto Diavolo, with relishing sauce; new broiled devil, Mayonnaise sauce; chicken, American fashion.

Stewed oysters on toast; ditto American fashion, au gratin; fried oysters.

Omelettes with fine herbs, mushrooms, sprue grass, ham, and parmesan; poached eggs with cream; ditto with maître d'hôtel sauce; semi-curried, with ham or bacon.

Buttered eggs with mushrooms, sprue grass, ham with shalots, parsley, and chervil.

Mirrored eggs with tongue, ham, or bacon; curried eggs; ditto with onion sauce and tomato sauce.

Rarebit à la Soyer with sherry or champagne.

Fried potatoes in slices; ditto with maître d'hôtel butter; ditto with Cayenne pepper.

Cold asparagus salad, while in season; new potato salad, German fashion; ditto, French and haricot beans.

*

A Hansom cab was waiting at the door, so I jumped in.

'Beg your pardon, sir, I am engaged,' said cabby; 'but if you're not going far, I think I shall have plenty of time to take you.'

'Do so, my man; I live close by, in Bloomsbury Street, Bedford Square. Here's a shilling for you – go ahead, cabby.'

Pst! pst! and off we were. In a few minutes, thanks to the evaporation of the thick fog and its having left only a feeble skeleton of its former substance, I found myself at my street door, and was trying for some time to open it with the wrong key, all the while thinking to myself what an extraordinary and uncomfortable evening I had passed to return so late. Perceiving my mistake, I changed the key; opening and shutting the door violently, I rushed upstairs with the intention of booking that evening in my daily tablet as one of the most tedious and uncomfortable I had spent throughout the series of cheerful years granted to me by a Supreme Power. The fire was out, the supper divided between my two friends the Angola cats, the servants in bed, the gas turned off, and the lucifers, I believe, gone to their Mephistophelian domain.

Off to the War

Messrs. Smith and Phillips, according to promise, brought me a most beautiful small model of the field stove, which they warranted first-rate, and to be capable of working in or out of doors, and in all weathers. I immediately proceeded to the War Office, to show the model, and explain the principle to Lord Panmure. In the waiting-room I had the honour of meeting the Duke of Cambridge, which gave me an excellent opportunity of explaining its merits. The Duke appeared to approve of it, and particularly noticed the great economy of fuel consequent upon the construction and smallness of the furnace. The Duke made some important remarks, and gave me a few hints upon the cooking regulations both in the hospitals and in the camps. These I took note of, and after explaining my plan of transport, I was quite delighted at having had such an opportunity of conversing with the Duke on a subject in which I was aware he felt particular interest. Mr. Ramsay, the secretary, having sent for me, I quitted the Duke; and, before leaving, I informed him that I had seen my friend Comte, and that he had given me all the assistance in his power, and had also told me that his highness had presented the hospital with a very nice *petite batterie de cuisine*, which, no doubt, I should find very useful upon my arrival.

'Adieu, Monsieur Soyer, I wish you well, and hope you will succeed.'

On reaching Mr. Ramsay's office, that gentleman kindly informed me that if I wished to see Lord Panmure I had better wait till he went to take his luncheon. I then stated that my object was to show his lordship the model of a stove I had invented for the use both of the hospitals and the army.

'Walk into the next room; Lord Panmure will be there in a few minutes, and you will have plenty of time to show it without interfering with his business.'

I had not waited ten minutes before Lord Panmure came in alone.

'Ah, Mr. Soyer, what have you there?'

'The model of a stove I wish to submit to your lordship. It is one which will, I believe, suit admirably for cooking both in and out of doors.'

After closely examining it, and listening to the details I had previously given to the Duke of Cambridge, Lord Panmure approved of it, and requested me to have another made, which he might keep by him for inspection.

He then inquired how many cooks I should take with me.

'Only a few from Paris,' I replied, 'as I wish to make a trial before engaging many people; besides, I hope to be able, in a very short time, to instruct the soldiers, who, being under discipline, might prove as useful as any cooks.'

Lord Panmure seemed pleased at my anxiety to instruct the soldiers; and, as he very justly remarked – 'We want them to learn how to cook their rations to the best advantage, and that your instructions should remain for ever among them. Well, I have settled all you wished me to do; and my secretary, Mr. Ramsay, will remit you all the letters you require. When do you think of starting?'

'By the next mail.'

'Well!' said his lordship, shaking me heartily by the hand, 'Goodbye, if I do not see you again before your departure.'

'It would only be troubling you; I therefore beg to take this opportunity of thanking your lordship for the kind reception and encouragement I have received, and, still more, for the confidence with which you have honoured me. I assure you that it will cause me to be most careful and economical, and it will be my pride to improve the diet without increasing the expense to Government. This may not be effected at first; but when the system is once introduced, and fairly established, I will answer for both a great amelioration as well as a saving.'

'I am confident, Soyer, that you will do your best.'

'Your lordship may depend upon me for that, were it only for my own sake.'

'Well, write as soon as you arrive, and let us know how you get on.'

Upon leaving, I met Mr. Ramsay, and related to him *verbatim* what had passed between Lord Panmure and myself. I then showed him the model, which he understood perfectly well, and gave me the engineer, Mr. Brunel's, address. I called upon that gentleman, and had the pleasure of an interview. He at once gave his full and entire approval of the principle, saying, 'You really come at a most propitious time; Dr. Mayne and myself are actually busily engaged discussing a plan for establishing kitchens in the Smyrna hospital. Yours will answer very well, and assist us materially, as it is always a tedious department to construct in order to be effective, and work properly. No doubt they will be applicable to every public institution; besides, what a small quantity of fuel they must consume.'

'Very little, indeed; and with this simple regulator you may manage the ebullition to a nicety, even in the open air. I shall also beg to remark, that they will be made of a beautiful metal, that will never require tinning; and the whole, though light in weight, will be extremely strong, and will last several years without needing repairs, or, at least, very trifling ones, that will not interfere with their use for a single day. They will take up but little room, and may be easily kept clean. No bricks are required, no chimney to be swept, and they can be as easily removed as any piece of furniture in your room.'

'You are perfectly right; and I give you my candid opinion, they are the very stoves required for the purpose. I should like Dr. Mayne to see it; if you can, call as you go to the War Office, and show him the model. I can then speak with him upon the subject.'

'With the greatest of pleasure.'

As Dr. Mayne had not arrived when I called, I went and fetched a passport for myself, and one for my secretary. Upon my return, the doctor had examined the model, and seemed much pleased, saying – 'It will answer very well.' I left the address of the manufacturers with him, and then retired. They were immediately adopted both at Smyrna, and later at Rankioi.

A gentleman present, who seemed to have taken a great deal of interest in our descriptive conversation, followed me to the door, and, in a low voice, asked if I had taken out a patent.

'No, I have not; but I shall put my name and label upon them.'

'Well, if you were to take out a patent, you would make a fortune.'

'You may be right; but upon such an occasion I should fancy myself wrong. I will therefore give it, *pro bono publico*. I am well aware that by making it more complete I could take out either registration or patent, but I would not do that for the world; as it would be immediately reported that I expected to be repaid for my services by the profits of the patent of the stove, and upon these grounds I decline any such proceeding.'

As it was then about three o'clock, I went, by appointment, to Sir Benjamin Hawes's office to bid that gentleman adieu, and to receive his final orders, showing him at the same time the model, which he seemed to appreciate thoroughly. He gave me the best advice, and promised me his powerful support throughout my culinary campaign. In return, I engaged to communicate all my movements, and retired.

At noon, next day, I again called at Stafford House, 'not by appointment.' On being informed of my visit, the Duchess at once favoured me with an audience. 'I am come,' said I, 'to announce my departure. I wish, ere I leave tomorrow, to thank your Grace, and to show you the model of my new stove which I mean to introduce into the hospital kitchens.'

'Ah!' exclaimed her Grace, 'I must go and fetch the Duke. He will be highly pleased with it, and he wished very much to see you before your departure.'

The Duke soon entered the great hall, with a large party, to whom I explained the principle, as I had before done to the Duke of Cambridge. I also stated that the day previous I had had the honour of showing it to Lord Panmure, and Mr. Brunel, the celebrated engineer, all of whom were much pleased with its efficacy, simplicity, and economy; more especially Mr. Brunel, who so highly appreciated the principle of its construction, that he at once adopted it, and applied it to the hospital kitchens at Smyrna and Rankioi, which he was there about to fit up.

The Duke made many remarks respecting the simplicity of its construction and the immense economy of fuel, 'the transport of which,' I observed, 'was so extremely difficult and costly.' I also remarked that one stove might be placed in a tent or hut containing fifty or sixty men; and they could cook there without the smallest inconvenience or difficulty, while it would throw out sufficient heat, 'being in use nearly all day, viz., for breakfast, dinner, and tea,' to warm the hut in winter, while in summer it might be turned out of doors.

Having been complimented by all present, I was about to retire, when the Duchess observed that she had written several letters of introduction for me. 'Among the number,' said her Grace, 'you will find one for Miss Nightingale.'

I returned my sincere thanks to all present, and in

particular to the Duke and Duchess. I assured them that the kindness and great encouragement I had received from them would be for ever engraved in my memory. The Duke remarked that he was very glad to see me in such high spirits. I acknowledged this with a bow.

'But, Mr. Soyer, suppose you should be taken ill?' said the Duchess.

'Well, your Grace – *cela est à la volonté de Dieu* – at present I am happy to say I have not any fears on that head, and am quite resigned to whatever Providence may dictate. Once more I beg to reiterate my feelings of gratitude, and bid your Grace and your illustrious family adieu.'

As it was nearly one o'clock, I called upon Mr. Ramsay, who had all my letters ready. He did me the honour to introduce me to General Vivian, of the Turkish Contingent, and his brother, Captain Ramsay, the general's aide-de-camp. Anticipating the pleasure of meeting those gentlemen in the East, I departed with the best wishes of all.

Mr. Ramsay gave me a letter for the Honourable Mrs. Herbert, to whom I was anxious to pay a visit, well aware of the important information I could gather from that benevolent lady, who was in constant communication with the hospitals in the East, and also with Miss Nightingale. I was very kindly received; but, instead of giving me an encouraging prospect of success, that lady very candidly informed me that the number of letters she daily received were most unsatisfactory, and that she did not think it possible for me to restore order in the cooking department at the great barrack hospital.

'The difficulties you will encounter,' said she, 'are incalculable.'

'So I anticipate,' was my reply; 'but I must observe, that I love difficulties, in order to surmount them. And with the power so graciously conferred upon me by Lord Panmure, I cannot fail to do some good, if my health does not fail me.'

'I hope,' said Mrs. Herbert, 'you will succeed, and shall be happy to hear of an amelioration. When do you think of going?'

'Tomorrow.' Bidding her adieu, and thanking her for her kind reception, I retired.

A Tour Round the Kitchen

At half-past six the next morning I was in the kitchen. The soldiers were at that hour making the coffee and tea for breakfast. I went with the serjeant on duty to inspect the quality of the meat, the quantity allowed, and the place of distribution. I found the meat of a very inferior quality, the method of distribution too complicated. When the weight of the quantity allowed was explained to me I found it correct. I was at first much puzzled at finding that some patients upon full diet received three quarters of a pound, some half a pound, and some a quarter of a pound of meat, accordingly as they were placed upon full, half, or quarter diet allowance – a system unavoidable in a hospital, but which would deceive the best cook. On some days, in providing for a hundred patients, this would make a difference of from ten to twenty pounds of meat, according to the number of half or quarter diets. Yet the same quantity of soup would nevertheless be required.

I made a note of this, and next perceived that every mess took their meat separately. Some messes numbered fifteen, twenty, or even thirty. The meat was spitted upon a rough piece of wood about two feet long, and then tied as tight as possible with a strong cord. Although this was a very bad method, I did not choose to interfere, as it was important for me to show them the evil effects of their system, and ensure a reform by pointing out a better. We then went to the store-rooms, and looked over what the contractor called the mixed vegetables, though they were principally of one kind, and half of these unfit for use. After having seen the rations weighed, I sent orders to the cooks not to commence operations until I arrived. We examined all kinds of preserved meats, soups, sweet-meats, &c. I next went to see the poultry, which I found of very inferior quality, consisting principally of old fowls, badly plucked and drawn. The gizzards, heads, and feet, which make such good broth, were thrown away. Mr. Bailey, whom I had not yet seen, then entered. When I had explained what we had already done, and the plan it would be most advisable to adopt for the future, he promised to bring the contractor, that we might talk the matter over. I examined the bread, which was very good indeed.

Mr. Bailey accompanied me to the various kitchens, where I had ordered the men to proceed as usual, and the same in the extra-diet kitchen. During our progress I had the pleasure of meeting and being introduced to most of the medical gentlemen as they were visiting the patients in the corridors and wards. Having been informed that Mr. Milton, the purveyor-in-chief, had arrived, I called at his office, but unfortunately he had just gone to some store-room – no one could tell which. I left my compliments, and a message to say that I should call again. I went to see Dr. Cumming, and report progress, and engaged to let him taste some of my cooking the following day. My next visit was to Lord W. Paulet, whom I found surrounded by military gentlemen of all ranks. He called me in, and, in a most good-natured manner, intro-duced me to his visitors, saying, 'Now M. Soyer is come, I fear he will feed the sick soldiers so well, that they will be sorry to recover and leave the hospital.'

'Should such prove to be the case, it will be the best of all bad complaints.'

Some of the company inquired whether I was going to the Crimea.

'I must first make my *début* here,' was my reply, 'and then we shall see.'

'Monsieur Soyer, what can I do for you?'

'Your lordship can do what I require in two minutes. Will you be kind enough to send me a carpenter or two, and a bricklayer, to do some little matters I wish to have attended to?'

'Certainly; I will drop a line to Captain Gordon, the chief engineer, to that effect. His office is over the way – you had better go and see him.'

'Captain Gordon,' said a soldier, who brought some letters, 'is gone to Pera.'

'I am happy to be able to inform your lordship that I am progressing very fast, and that everyone is very obli-ging to me.'

'I am glad to hear that, Monsieur Soyer.'

'I suppose you could not spare time about one o'clock, to go round and see the meals served out?'

'I will try; but I fear I shall hardly have leisure. See what I have to do,' he continued, pointing to a pile of letters which the soldier had just brought in; 'as Doctor Macgregor is going round with you, he will give me an account of everything.'

It was then noon, and about dinner-time. So I returned to the kitchen, where all was in the greatest confusion. Such a noise I never heard before. They were waiting for their soup and meat, and using coarse language, without making the least progress in the distribution. The market at old Billingsgate, during the first morning sale, was nothing compared to this military row. Each man had two tin cans for the soup. They kept running about and knocking against each other, in most admirable disorder. Such confusion, thought I, is enough to kill a dozen patients daily. As a natural consequence, several must go without anything; as, owing to the confusion, some of the orderly waiters get more and others less than their allowance. Any attempt to alter this at the time, would have been as wise as endeavouring to stop the current of the Bosphorus. As I did not wish to lose the chance of seeing the rations served out in the wards, I went for Dr. Macgregor, and we called for Mr. Milton – but the latter had not returned. I then fetched Miss Nightingale, and we went through the wards. The process of serving out the rations, though not quite such a noisy scene as that I had before witnessed, was far from being perfect. In the first place, the patients were allowed to eat the meat before the soup. As I was confident that this could not be by the doctor's order, I asked the reason. The reply was, 'we have only one plate.' (What they called a plate, was a round and deep tin dish, which held a pound of meat and a pint of soup.) I therefore recommended them to cut the meat as usual into small pieces, and pour the pint of boiling soup over it. This method had the advantage of keeping the meat hot.

'It will enable the patients,' I said, 'to eat both the soup and meat warm, instead of cold – the daily practice, in consequence of the slow process of carving.'

'Very true,' said Dr. Macgregor. 'Nay, more, the soup will comfort and dispose the stomach for the better digestion of the meat and potatoes. When the men are very hungry, they will often swallow their food without properly masticating it, and the meat is also probably tough.'

We then tasted both the soup and meat. The former was thin and without seasoning; the latter, mutton, tough and tasteless. The potatoes were watery. All these defects I promised to rectify the next day. We proceeded to a ward where they complained bitterly that the meat was never done; in fact, it was quite raw, and then of course the cook was blamed.

'Now,' said I to Miss Nightingale, 'I will wager anything that we shall find some parts very well done, and some, no doubt, too much done, though it is all cooked in the same caldron.'

'How do you account for that, Monsieur Soyer? is it owing to the bad quality of the meat?'

'Not at all; that may come from the same sheep, and yet vary.'

At another mess, the meat was well done, a small piece at the end only being over-cooked.

'I will explain this to you, madam,' said I. 'I remarked this morning that the man tied all the joints together very tight, after having put them upon a "skewer," as he calls it, almost as large as a wooden leg. The consequence is, that when the meat is thrown into boiling water, it is not properly done; the meat swells, and it is impossible for the heat or the water even to get at it.'

'Ah, I noticed that several of the men did exactly as you say this morning,' said Miss Nightingale. 'The parts which are well done were placed loose upon the stick; and this explains the mystery – but I shall alter that tomorrow.'

Having afterwards inspected several extra-diet kitchens, and tasted various things, I perceived what I could accomplish, both as regarded convalescents and extra diets. Miss Nightingale having again offered to render any assistance in her power, left us, as she had a great deal to attend to. I retraced my steps to Dr. Cumming's, and stated my opinion of the present system of cooking; and explained what I proposed doing, of all of which he approved highly. I then returned to the kitchen, and sent a requisition for six rations of everything allowed for making the soup. I proceeded thus: –

To eight pints of water I put four pounds of meat, a quarter of a pound of barley, a little salt and pepper, and the allowance of vegetables, and in about an hour I produced a very good soup – some of which I sent to several doctors. They tasted and praised it highly, as being very nourishing and palatable. I then carried some to Dr. Cumming, who approved of its composition; but expressed his opinion that it would probably be too expensive. I then informed him I had made it with the ration allowance, taking the meat at half-diet scale. He was much pleased with the meat, which he pronounced highly palatable, and thought that the seasoning should be put in with the other ingredients. I explained that I could still improve it by the simple addition of a small quantity of sugar and flour.

'The purveyor will not, I am certain, refuse that,' said he.

'Oh, I am aware of that; but I wish to manage it without increasing the expense. I must accomplish that, if possible.' Miss Nightingale and Dr. Macgregor, to both of whom I sent some, praised it even more than the others had done, particularly the meat, which they stated to be of a very excellent flavour, and they had the opportunity of tasting the former. Mr. Milton came in, and though I had not had the pleasure of seeing that gentleman, from the description I had heard of him, and his pleasing manner, I knew I was not mistaken in saying – 'Mr. Milton, allow me to have the honour of tendering my best compliments and thanks for your prompt visit.'

'No person could be more welcome here than you are, Monsieur Soyer. I only regret I was not in my office when you called. I should have been happy to have accompanied you round the wards. Your very just remarks have been repeated to me and the plan you mean to adopt explained, but I fear you will meet with so many difficulties that you will get tired before you have achieved much good.'

'Not at all,' I replied; 'you will see a great change by tomorrow, which must be attributed chiefly to the politeness and cordial assistance I have met with from the members of every department – especially your own – which to me is the most important.'

'I have given orders that everything you may require is to be placed at your disposal, if in store; and any alteration or suggestion which is likely to be beneficial will be immediately attended to. You have only to ask for anything you need in the way of cooking utensils, and it shall, if possible, be procured.'

'My great object and delight will be to effect a change with the daily allowance.'

'That would certainly be as well; but I fancy it cannot be done. The provisions here are of a quality very inferior to what we get in London.'

'You are quite right, if they are all like those I saw this morning. Favour me by tasting these two soups. Julien! please to give Mr. Milton two small basins of soup – one of mine, and one of that made at the hospital.' On tasting mine first he pronounced it very good and palatable, and of an excellent flavour. The other, although made with exactly the same materials, he could hardly swallow. It had no seasoning, had a blackish appearance, and was quite tasteless.

'There is no comparison,' said Mr. Milton.

'All the soup will in future be like the sample I have made, and I can greatly improve it by the addition of a few pounds of brown sugar and a little flour extra.'

'Monsieur Soyer, I beg you will not regard such trivial expenses, at any rate for the present; what is required you shall have.'

'I see the fresh vegetables are very bad – as you have a quantity of preserved ones, I shall mix them.'

'In future we must try and get better meat, poultry, and eggs; and, above all, charcoal. I am aware you have justly complained of them. Have you seen our bread?'

'Yes, I have, and very good it is too.'

'That is really all we can manage to my satisfaction. As regards the meat and poultry, I will send you the contractor; but the charcoal is in the commissariat department. I shall write an official letter respecting it. I see,' he continued, looking at some, 'it is all dust, and seems quite wet.'

'Pray send off a letter; and if you will give me the name of the gentleman who is at the head of that department, I shall be happy to make his acquaintance; and beg of him not to allow any delay, as I consider this the most important matter of all.'

I repeated the reason for saying this which I have before mentioned.

After listening attentively to my remarks, Mr. Milton said, –

'You may well call it the most important, and the sooner it is altered the better.'

We parted. I then told the soldier-cooks to have the boilers thoroughly cleaned, and everything in from the stores by eight o'clock the next morning, as I intended making the soup myself. I left Julien, my head man, with them to superintend matters.

Having called upon Doctor Taylor, I had a long conversation with him upon cookery. In the course of this he said, –

'On finding that the cooking was so badly done, I took upon myself, not only to superintend the men, but also to cook and teach them; and I must say I found them very willing. How could I expect them to know anything about it? they had never been taught to do it.'

'True, Doctor; and, as soon as they begin to know a

little about it, they are recalled to their regiments, and replaced by newcomers as ignorant as they were themselves at first.'

'Exactly; and I tell you what, Monsieur Soyer, though we may be very good doctors, and possess a thorough knowledge of medical science, we still need the aid of culinary science; for the one without the other will produce but very unsatisfactory results. Since I have turned my attention to it, I am more and more fortified in the opinion which I have expressed before several medical boards, that a doctor, to be well qualified, should have some knowledge of the art of cookery, and this he ought to acquire in the first stage of his medical education.'

'Indeed, Doctor, it is not with the view of elevating my profession, to which I have now devoted my attention for more than twenty-seven years, that I say I am persuaded that this science has been too lightly treated. In corroboration of your just remark, I have, as you will find, already stated in my various works upon cookery, that to make a good cook it is of paramount importance that a man should possess some chemical as well as medical knowledge.'

'I agree with you, Monsieur Soyer,' said he.

'As soon as my kitchen is ready, Doctor, I hope you will favour me with a visit.'

'With much pleasure. Let me know when it is finished.'

To my great regret, I was obliged to see about returning to Pera, some delay having taken place in the completion of my house. On reaching the landing-place not a caique was to be had, the weather was so bad they could not cross. A friend offered me shelter for that night at a small restaurant kept by a Greek called Demetri. There were seventeen of us lying on straw sofas, with the privilege of covering ourselves with our greatcoats, if fortunate enough to possess one. Rooms were at a premium in Scutari. It was also necessary for anybody who wished to have the benefit of his greatcoat to keep awake all night; for no sooner did you begin to doze than some of your sleeping partners, who happened to be wide awake, endeavoured to appropriate the coveted garment to their use; and the weather being very chilly, this proved anything but pleasant. Unfortunately, after passing an uncomfortable night, I did not feel much refreshed, and was almost unfit to undertake the difficult task I had before me. However, I was up at six, and in the kitchen by seven. None of my orders had been attended to. My own people were not there as they ought to have been; and the men told me they could not get the rations till ten o'clock, that being the usual time for issuing them.

'Really,' said I; 'and pray who told you so?'

'The serjeant and some of the orderlies,' was the reply.

'We shall see all about that; come with me.'

The truth is, I did find it very difficult to get anything; but, in less than half-an-hour after I had been to the purveyor's headquarters my new regiment began to manœuvre admirably under my command. By eight o'clock everything was ready for the cooking, except my cooks, who had been sleeping in a store-room upon some straw, and had a regular fray with the allied rats. These animals, it appears, had come to welcome them to Scutari.

Upon inspecting the boilers, my first fear was

realized – there was nothing but copper – all the tinning had worn away. And very difficult was it to ascertain this fact, these immense and deep caldrons being securely screwed to the marble basement, and extremely difficult, not only to remove, but also to tin when removed. I consider it most advisable that all large establishments should have their cooking apparatus made of malleable iron, which is extremely clean, is much cheaper, and does not require tinning: the lid may be made of copper for appearance' sake, but not so the boiler. The kitchen battery of the wealthy alone should be copper, as they can afford to employ professional persons for the preparation of their diet, who never would attempt using them when coppery.

That day I was obliged to use them. Having put the proper quantity of water into each copper, with the meat, barley, vegetables, and salt and pepper, we lighted the fires; and after allowing the ingredients to simmer for two hours and a half, an excellent soup was made; I only adding a little sugar and flour to finish it.

The receipt for this excellent soup, so highly approved of and immediately adopted by the medical men, will be found in my Hospital Diets, with a scale of proportions from ten to a hundred.

The meat was so poor that there was no fat to skim off the soup. It was therefore served out at once, as described in the receipt. Several doctors went round with me, and asked the men how they liked it. They were all highly delighted with it, and praised it very much. I also took care that the rations of meat should not be tied together on the skewer.

The orderlies were now ordered not to tie their rations of meat so tight. Upon inspection I found that they had a most curious method of marking their different lots. Some used a piece of red cloth cut from an old jacket; others half a dozen old buttons tied together; old knives, forks, scissors, &c., but one in particular had hit upon an idea which could not fail to meet with our entire approval. The discovery of this brilliant idea was greeted with shouts of laughter from Miss Nightingale, the doctors, and myself. It consisted in tying a pair of old snuffers to the lot.

All this rubbish was daily boiled with the meat, but probably required more cooking. On telling the man with the snuffers that it was a very dirty trick to put such things in the soup, the reply was – 'How can it be dirty, sir? sure they have been boiling this last month.'

When all the dinners had been served out, I perceived a large copper half full of rich broth with about three inches of fat upon it. I inquired what they did with this?

'Throw it away, sir.'

'Throw it away?' we all exclaimed.

'Yes, sir; it's the water in which the fresh beef has been cooked.'

'Do you call that water? I call it strong broth. Why don't you make soup of it?'

'We orderlies don't like soup, sir.'

'Then you really do throw it away?'

'Yes, sir; it is good for nothing.'

I took a ladle and removed a large basinful of beautiful fat, which, when cold, was better for cooking purposes than the rank butter procured from Constantinople at from ten to fifteen piastres per pound. The next day I showed the men how to make a most delicious soup with what they had before so foolishly thrown away. This method they were henceforward very glad to adopt. Not less than seventy pounds of beef had been daily boiled in this manner, and without salt. It would hardly be credited, but for its truth I can appeal to Miss Nightingale and others who were present.

Nothing was needed but a sharp look-out after the cooks in order to ensure complete success. The day after I had the coppers tinned. The next thing was to have a charcoal stove built, an oven, a store-room, and a larder partitioned off; and a kitchen dresser and chopping-block made. Through the kindness of the Chief Engineer, Captain Gordon, these things were accomplished in a few days, and at a trifling expense. If not a very magnificent, it was, as will be seen, a very spacious and handy kitchen.

In a few days I made experiments in small quantities upon all the various extra diets, such as chicken, mutton, and veal broth, the cooking of fowls, beef and mutton tea, &c. I did not forget the beverages, such as rice water, lemonades, arrowroot, panada ditto, barley water, sago jelly, &c.; rice pudding, sago, bread, vermicelli and macaroni ditto. The receipts will be found in the Addenda, under the head of 'Hospital Diets.'

A gentleman, Mr. Black, who was a first-class interpreter, was then introduced to me by the Purveyor-in-Chief, and appointed to assist me in any way I might require his aid. He was highly recommended by Miss Nightingale, and a number of first-class doctors, as well as by Lord William Paulet. It is with gratitude that I acknowledge the great assistance I received from that gentleman during his stay with me, and the energy he displayed in procuring everything I required. He spoke French fluently, also the Turkish, Greek, and Armenian languages. This rendered him invaluable to me, as I was obliged to employ people speaking those different languages in my numerous kitchens. And what was more remarkable still, he was the husband of the celebrated Maid of Athens, whose company I had the pleasure of enjoying several times; and although this interesting personage is now in her tenth lustre, some remains of the great Byron seem still engraved on the physiognomy of the once celebrated Greek beauty; and she informed me that when Lord Byron wrote his poem on her, she was but ten years of age, he at the time residing opposite the house of her parents at Athens.

Three Weeks at Scutari

[. . .]

My long-expected field stoves had arrived. I made a trial with them before the military and medical authorities, which succeeded admirably, even surpassing my expectations in all respects. I was more anxious than ever to return to the Crimea, and make my grand experiment before General Simpson; and, if approved of by the authorities, to have the proper number ordered by Government for the supply of the whole army, reform the old system, and introduce my new one. The stoves would of course require an outlay at first, which would soon be saved in the great economy of fuel and transport, and the small number of men required, independently of the immense improvement in cookery, which was at first the only object I had in view.

Lord W. Paulet's visit took place, as agreed upon, about three days previous to the arrival of the Duke of Newcastle. He found everything in good order, and I was much pleased. A few days after, I was, owing to the sudden departure of my head man, Julien, busily engaged at my forges, surrounded by my soldiers, like a modern Vulcan, dressed in my culinary attire, and in the act of manipulating some hundreds of *mock rice puddings* (made without eggs or milk – see pp. 89–90) for my numerous convalescent guests, the brave British, when suddenly my kitchen was filled with military gentlemen of all ranks, amongst whom was no less a personage than the late Minister-at-war, the Duke of Newcastle, Lord W. Paulet, and numerous other high officials – military, medical, and civil. His Grace, setting all etiquette aside, advanced towards me, his hat in one hand, and kindly offered me the other, saying, 'How are you, Monsieur Soyer? it is a long time since we had the pleasure of meeting.'

'True,' I replied; 'not since I had the pleasure of seeing your Grace, then Lord Lincoln, at the Reform Club.'

'You are right, Monsieur Soyer; you have an excellent memory.'

Though my present occupation was one of the humblest in the category of my art, – viz., making puddings for the soldiers, still the kind condescension of his Grace, and the complimentary remarks he made upon my services, caused me to feel more proud of my humble occupation than I did when I was dressing the great Ibrahim Pacha fête at the Reform Club, in the year 1846, or preparing my hundred-guinea dish at the York banquet, in the year 1850.

The Duke of Newcastle was not the first nobleman of his high rank who had honoured me with that degree of favour; but the others had a certain interest in so doing. For instance, while at the Reform Club, a number of epicures used to pay me visits, shake me heartily by the hand, and most cordially inquire about my health. These had, I always considered, a twofold object in view: first, to induce me to give them the best of dinners; secondly, to ascertain whether I was feverish or in good health. In the former case they would postpone their dinner-party for a few days, or else try to persuade me to follow the plan of the celebrated Marquis de Coucy, one of the greatest French epicures of the nineteenth century, who never engaged a cook without having a written agreement, giving him power to compel him to take medicine a couple of days before he gave any of his grand dinners, which never exceeded twelve in the Paris season. Extra pay was allowed for this pleasant concession on the part of the *chef de cuisine*, who no doubt turned the funds to *tisane* – most probably, *tisane de champagne*.

In the present case, his Grace had no such object in view, as I had nothing to offer him but soldiers' hospital rations, diets, &c., composed of beef-tea, mutton-broth, rice puddings, &c., and my new biscuit-bread, which had been made three months, having the date of baking stamped upon it. I drew the Duke's attention to this, and then broke a little into some mutton-broth; and in five minutes it had all the appearance of a piece of fresh bread soaked in broth. In its dry state, it was much more agreeable to eat than the usual biscuit. His Grace was highly pleased with it, and advised me to recommend its adoption to the War Office upon my return to London.

The kitchen was by this time full of officers and medical men, come to pay their respects to the Duke, forming a numerous escort as he went round the hospital. I gave a short account of my proceedings since my arrival at Scutari, where I had closed all the kitchens but this one, minutely explaining all its details, as well as the plan I had adopted to keep it so clean and so cool; at which the Duke was much struck. Cooking was done daily in it for more than one thousand men, the weather being then intensely hot. After honouring me with most flattering compliments, the Duke and party retired. Lord William kindly informed me that the Duke would visit the other hospitals in a day or two, and that he would give me due notice of his visit. Accordingly, two days afterwards, we showed the Duke over the General, Hyder Pacha, and the Palace Hospitals, with the arrangements of which he expressed himself satisfied.

A few days after, the Duke of Newcastle left for the Crimea, but, prior to his departure, honoured me with the following letter: –

MESSERIE'S HOTEL, *23rd July, 1855.*
DEAR M. SOYER, – Accept my best thanks for the copy of your book.
Your philanthropic labours in this country deserve the thanks of every Englishman, and for one I am grateful for what I have seen of your good work at Scutari.
I am, yours very truly,
NEWCASTLE.

At length I found two tolerably good cooks, and re-established everything in the culinary department to my satisfaction. My presence being no longer required, I prepared for my departure. I had taught about a dozen soldiers my system of camp-cooking and the use of my new field stoves. I also engaged a French Zouave, named Bornet, belonging to the 3rd Regiment, whose term of service was just out. He was to act as my aide-de-camp, écuyer, master of the horse, and shield, in case of blows. He knew the savate, single-stick, sword, foil, and could box well; was a capital shot and extraordinary good horseman; he could sing hundreds of songs, and very well too; had a good voice, danced excellently, and was altogether of a very happy disposition.

Among his other then unknown qualities, he was very quarrelsome; a great marauder *à la* Zouave; remarkably fond of the fair sex, in his martial way, running all over the camp after the heroic *cantinières*; and, though never drunk, seldom sober, always ready to fight anyone who he thought wished to injure or speak ill of me. In fact, he was, much against my will, my bulldog, and kept barking from morning till night. He was allowed to wear his costume for twelve months longer. In fact, my Zouave was a model of perfection and imperfection. The doctor of his regiment, who admired him for his bravery and cheerful abilities, impressed upon me that he was the man I required. 'Very scarce they are,' said he; 'there are not more than one hundred left out of the whole regiment who began the campaign; and he is sound, although wounded at Inkermann.'

Upon this strong recommendation, and having to run so much risk about the camp, as well as for the curiosity of the thing, I engaged Bornet, the Zouave; had a new costume made for him; introduced him to Lord W. Paulet, Miss Nightingale, &c. &c. Everybody found him extremely polite, good-looking, and intelligent. We bought four horses, and he had the sole command of the cavalry department. All admired his extraordinary good style of horsemanship, particularly Lord W. Paulet. Thus, the illustrious François Patifal Bornet, late of the 3rd Zouaves, was recognised as belonging to the British army. He and twelve soldiers composed the brigade of Captain Cook – a title I had assumed in the camp.

We were now ready to enter upon our campaign. I had paid my respects to Lord and Lady de Redcliffe at Therapia, and to General Vivian at Buyukderé: he was then at the Palais de Russie. In this town I and my Zouave created quite a sensation. I had adopted an indescribable costume. It seemed to have attracted John Bull's particular attention on his supposed visit to the camp. Such, at least, was the case according to the *Times* correspondent, who, in a dialogue with John Bull, says, 'I beg your pardon, but who is that foreign officer in a white bournous and attended by a brilliant staff of generals – him with the blue and silver stripe down his trousers I mean, and gold braid on his waistcoat, and a red and white cap? It must be Pelissier?'

'That! why, that's Monsieur Soyer, *chef de nos batteries de cuisine*; and if you go and ask him, you'll find he'll talk to you for several hours about the way your meat is wasted. And so I wish you good morning, sir.'

Camp Life at Headquarters

As Bornet was a dashing cavalier and a very good horse-man, he created quite a sensation in Kadikoi, and upon our arrival before the Sardinian headquarters, General della Marmora and staff came upon the balcony to look at him. He saluted the general, who appeared much sur-prised to see a Zouave on horseback in my suite, and not wearing the exact costume of that corps, as I had made some stylish improvement in it, in order to distinguish him from the common soldiers.

As I had to see General Simpson about eleven o'clock, off we went at full gallop, being rather short of time. Mrs. Seacole, who was at her door with her daughter Sarah, had only time to call out, 'Go it, my sons!' as we rattled past the house. We arrived in due time, and I saw Colonel Steele, who told me that General Simpson would be happy to receive me directly, and at once conducted me to his audience-chamber. The new Commander-in-chief rose politely as I entered, shook me by the hand, and invited me to be seated. I had previously left a letter for him from Lord William Paulet respecting my mission, and I showed two I had received from the War Office, in which the Minister-at-War expressed in flattering terms his approbation of them.

After the usual compliments of a first interview, General Simpson told me that he had read the letter with great interest, and would give me all the assistance in his power to enable me to carry out my project, which was, first, to make a trial before the commander-in-chief, the generals and officers of the army, Dr. Hall, &c. &c. If on that occasion my new system was approved of, it was my intention to introduce the same for the benefit of the army at large. To this General Simpson gave his assent, saying, 'You have only, Monsieur Soyer, to tell me what you require.'

'First of all, general, that you should select a spot where the trial can take place, and name a regiment with which I can begin.'

'You will require a building for your kitchen.'

'Not at all, general – no masons, carpenters, nor engineers. My stoves are adapted for the open air, to cook in all weathers, and to follow the army.'

'I am aware of that, as I saw the model when you were here last.'

'Exactly. All I shall require will be three bell-tents for myself and assistants, as I must reside in the camp.'

'Very well; I will give orders to that effect.'

'I would also recommend you to select a regiment near headquarters for your own convenience in visiting and watching the progress of the kitchens.'

'I think the Guards in the First Division will suit our purpose best. Do you know where they are?'

'I do; but perhaps you will be kind enough to send some official with me to select the spot.'

'We will ride over this afternoon. You had better dine with us this evening. You know the greater part of the gentlemen of my Staff; and those you do not, know you.'

'Many thanks, general, for your kind invitation, which I accept with the greatest pleasure.'

'Have you anything in that parcel to show me?'

'Yes; one of my new bread-biscuits, which I wish you to taste.'

On opening the parcel, he took it out, saying, 'Lord bless you! this will be too hard for my teeth.'

'Not so hard as you think. It is much softer than the ordinary biscuit which it is intended to replace. At any rate, it may be issued in turn, and will afford an excellent change for the troops. I have kept some above three months, and they are quite good. The Duke of Newcastle tasted one of them, and was much pleased with it.'

Having broken a piece off and tasted it, the general partook of some and found it very good, though not nearly so hard as he anticipated. He declared that it was much more palatable than the common biscuit, and that he quite enjoyed it. General Simpson was at that time very unwell, and he seldom ate anything but arrowroot and biscuit soaked in boiling water. I tasted some of his fare, and found it tolerably good, but not nutritive enough for a man who worked hard. He informed me that he was often occupied eight or ten hours a day writing. As his complaint was diarrhœa, I proposed boiling some plain rice after the receipt given in Addenda, which was at all times so much approved of by the doctors. This I did the next day. The general took a great deal of bodily exercise in the camp and in the trenches.

On quitting General Simpson, I paid my respects to General Eyre, with whom I had some business to transact. He was then at the head of the Ordnance Office, and

General Simpson had referred me to him for all I might require from that department. The general gave me a very kind reception, and granted all that I required. Having two hours to spare, I made up my mind to go to the French camp or headquarters. I had not had the pleasure of seeing General Pelissier since he received the appointment of commander-in-chief. As I was going out, I met General Jones, the engineer.

'Do you recollect, Monsieur Soyer, where we met last?'

Aware that the General – now Sir John Jones – was the siege and trench engineer, I thought that he referred to my wild expedition when I lost my way in the blood-stained labyrinth. I was, however, quite mistaken. He informed me that it was in Ireland, when I opened my kitchens in the year 1847. I then recollected the circumstance, as I had myself shown him round the kitchens, and explained the method and the process of cooking by steam for ten thousand people, if required, with only one furnace, and by means of steam-pipes connected with a double boiler – a plan, I believe, still in use in many large governmental and civil institutions.

I gave Sir John to understand what great pleasure it afforded me to hear of such reminiscences, and inquired if he intended to go for a ride as far as the First Division.

'No, Monsieur Soyer,' said he, 'I don't think I can. In fact, I have to be in the trenches, where I shall be happy to see you when you have fixed upon the spot for your field-kitchens.'

'I thank you, general, for your kind invitation, but would rather see you out of them, and a good distance off, particularly as a person is more exposed to the fire of the enemy on entering or leaving than when inside.'

Finding that I had hardly time to go as far as the French headquarters, I went to the kitchen and inquired what there was for dinner. The *chef* was named Nicolo, and had lived with Sir George Brown.

The horses were at the door in readiness for the general. All the Staff were in attendance before the house, some sitting on the steps, others standing. Among them were Generals Barnard and Airey, Colonels Steele and Blane, Captains Colville, Lindsay, &c., with whom I conversed upon various matters, especially upon my long stay at the Reform Club. General Barnard, as usual, was very talkative and witty.

When Colonel Steele saw General Simpson coming, he called to me to mount, and a few minutes after we set off to the First Division. On our way, we conversed upon various topics, particularly respecting a poor fellow named Harvey, who had been shot in his tent during the night. A ball from one of the enemy's long-rangers had fractured both his legs, and he died a few hours after receiving the wound. The most remarkable part of the occurrence, as I told the General, was this: – The person who usually occupied the spot got drunk the night before, and was put in the guardhouse: this saved his life. The ball made a hole about two feet deep at the very spot where he generally slept, every inch of room being turned to account in the tents. He must have been smashed to atoms, had he been there. The man who was killed had his legs close to this spot, and the shot falling in a slanting direction, cut them both off. The general said he had heard that a man had been killed during the night, but that he was not aware of the circumstances.

'On my way to the General Hospital,' I continued, 'in the morning, I saw the tent and the place where the cannon-ball fell. I have the piece of canvas the shot passed through; it was given me by Dr. Taylor of the Third Division, who took me to see it. It bears the name of the man killed and the date of the accident. The doctor, after cutting out the piece which was hanging to the tent, wrote the particulars upon it himself. I will show it to you this evening, general. My man has the relic with him.'

Some officers came and conversed with the general for a short time while we were before the Guards' camp. On the esplanade the men were parading for the trenches; there might have been four companies. The general spoke to the commanding officers, and they all started. A detachment of the Scots Fusiliers, headed by a band of music playing a lively tune, were returning from the funeral of one of their officers. This scene made a singular impression upon me. I was, in the first place, struck at seeing those fine fellows going, some probably to their doom – for who could tell how many would get back safely? – and in the second place, at the sight of the return of the funeral, playing such a joyous strain. This I learned, upon inquiry, was always the case after interring the corpse and leaving the cemetery.

One company had not started for the trenches. It was commanded by Colonel Seymour of the Guards, now aide-de-camp to H. R. H. Prince Albert. General Simpson, who had been some time talking with that officer, said to me, 'Monsieur Soyer, here is Colonel Seymour, who will render you any assistance you may require.'

'Much obliged, general.'

'Oh,' said the colonel, 'Monsieur Soyer and myself are old acquaintances. I often paid you a visit at the Reform Club.'

'Indeed, colonel!'

'Certainly – very often.'

Though the face was well known to me, I could not for the life of me recognise the colonel, he had such a large beard and mustachios. General Simpson then left us together, and I observed that I should give him as little trouble as possible, but for a short time should require all his kind assistance for the opening of my kitchen.

'You may depend upon me, Monsieur Soyer,' he said, – 'that is, if I return safe from the trenches.'

'I sincerely hope you may.'

'No one can tell. Thank God, I have been very fortunate so far.'

'I hope that you will continue to be so.'

We made an appointment. He started on horseback at the head of his men. I was introduced to numerous other officers by the general, and afterwards by the colonel, with many of whom I had the honour of being previously acquainted. Having selected a spot on the esplanade facing the centre avenue which divided the Coldstreams from the Scots Fusiliers, I returned alone to headquarters, it being then nearly dinner-time. My Zouave had got back from Balaklava, whither I had sent him to fetch my evening dress, in which I immediately attired myself, as dinner was upon the table. We sat down about twelve in number. As I was nearly opposite General Simpson, I had the opportunity of conversing with him upon various subjects. For a Crimean dinner, it was a very good one indeed. Colonel Steele and Captain Colville, who were sitting next me, attributed it to my presence, and said that the cook – Nicolo – had certainly distinguished himself upon the occasion.

'I am much pleased,' I replied, 'to be the cause of so great an improvement in the culinary department, and hope for the future the commander-in-chief will avail himself of my influence by often inviting me to dine at headquarters.'

After dinner, the evening passed very merrily, and the general cordially joined in the fun, though he seemed full of business, leaving the table several times to write despatches in his cabinet. We were smoking on the balcony at the back of the house, facing the vineyard, when the general returned from one of his short excursions, and I showed him the piece of canvas which I had obtained from my Zouave.

'Had the ball,' I said, 'fallen upon a stone, or anything offering resistance, it might have killed twenty men, as it fell in the thickest part of the Third Division. The deep hole it made in the tent was as polished and hard as the interior of a marble mortar. This was no doubt caused by the rapid revolutions of the ball in burying itself before its force was spent. I noticed this whilst looking at the cavity; and the men who were lying in the tent were of my opinion, and assured me that it kept making a tremendous noise for some time after its fall.'

While we were engaged in conversation I believe that

another despatch arrived, for the general and some of his Staff were called out. Observe, reader, that for a full hour the cannon and mortars had not ceased roaring throughout the camps, continually vomiting forth death and destruction on every side; yet everyone present, I as well as the rest, appeared quite indifferent to that mournful noise. We were, however, soon awakened by the fierce rattling of the fusillade. All listened attentively, but without moving from their seats. A message from the general and fresh orders caused us to break up the party. I was leaving the house, intending to return to Balaklava, when I met Major Lindsey, one of the aides-de-camp of General Simpson, entering with, I believe, another despatch. He asked me where I was going to sleep: I answered, at Balaklava.

'Oh, nonsense! don't go away. We are all ordered for half-past three in the morning. A great battle is expected, as the Russians are going to attack us upon a fresh point. I will give you a plank and a blanket in my room to lie upon for an hour or so.'

I accepted his kind offer, and he left me. When I informed my Zouave of the anticipated battle,

'By Jove!' said he, 'I hope they will give me a gun and sword to go and fight. I shall make a busy day of it. I smell powder. Pray, governor, do beg of the general to let me go with them.'

The fellow had taken a drop too much, and he went on like a madman – no one could check him. We retired to our hospitable abode, and I went to sleep; but the mad Zouave was anywhere and everywhere. At three o'clock I awoke. The general and his Staff started – the cannonade was going on fiercely, but no fusillade was heard. At seven the general and all returned; and it was, as he said, a false alarm.

My Zouave returned at eight, loaded with provisions, which he told me he had borrowed of some fellows he had found fast asleep. We arrived on board the *Baraguay d'Hilliers* about ten, faint with fatigue and hunger, having had no breakfast.

Such was camp-life at headquarters. It was like swimming between life and death. No one seemed to apprehend the least danger, while a successful sortie on the part of the enemy would have placed everyone's life in the greatest peril. So much for the unprofitable business of war!

Having fixed upon a spot for my kitchen, I immediately sent the stoves to the camp. As they happened to be close to the railway, they arrived early the next morning. In the course of the day I reached my field of battle, and to my great surprise found – what? Why, all my battery firing for the support of the Highland Brigade. The stoves had arrived early enough for the men to use them in cooking their dinners. Though I had given special orders that no one should meddle with them until I arrived, it gave me great pleasure to find that the men were using them to the best advantage and without instruction. In the first place, they could not possibly burn more than twenty pounds of wood in cooking for a hundred men, instead of several hundred-weight, which was the daily consumption. Although I had not given them my receipts, they found they could cook their rations with more ease, and hoped they should soon have them for everyday use, instead of the small tin camp-kettles, and their open-air system of cooking. The process was very unsatisfactory, being dependent upon good, bad, or indifferent weather, and the fuel was often wet and difficult to ignite. Colonel Seymour, whom I invited to see the men using the stoves without tuition from me or anybody else, can testify to the accuracy of this fact, having witnessed the process and interrogated them upon the subject.

My reason, reader, for relating this circumstance, is because it afforded me an assurance that I could render service to the army, and that my exertions were of some use. I saw even further than that; for I inferred that if a soldier, who is not a cooking animal, being paid for other purposes – and that talent a peculiar gift conferred in a greater or less degree upon humanity – could without trouble or instruction cook well in the open air and in all weathers, the stoves would certainly be useful in all establishments, from a cottage to a college. I do not say anything of their use in hospitals, because they had been tried in those establishments with full success, as far as military cooking was concerned. The idea of connecting baking, roasting, boiling, and steaming crossed my mind; and this, I felt with confidence, would render them beneficial and useful to the public at large. This idea I at once communicated to the makers, and they have already acted upon my suggestion. I resolved upon my return to England to bring them out at as cheap a rate as possible for the use of small or large families. A really useful and economical cooking stove is as much wanted in England as sunshine on a November day – a stove by which all the usual domestic cooking can be

carried on, without having recourse to bricks and mortar, and chimney-sweeps. Smoky chimneys, as well as
other minor nuisances too numerous to mention, would
be thus avoided. Twelve pounds of coal, or fifteen pounds
of coke, will cook for one hundred men.

'War,' said I to myself, 'is the evil genius of a time; but
good food for all is a daily and a paramount necessity.'
These reflections led to a further communication with
Messrs. Smith and Phillips, of Snow Hill. I took out a
patent for the stoves. This I did not like to do before I
had introduced them to the Government, as every one
would have supposed that I wished to make money by
the patent. The object of a patent, after such a decided
success, was to secure the solidity and perfection of the
article. As it was difficult to make, and certain to be
badly imitated, my reputation must have suffered.
Instead of being expensive, they will be sold at a reason-
able price, sufficient to repay the manufacturers, and to
leave a fair profit; thus placing them within the reach of
all – the million as well as the millionaire.

As the Highlanders had already used the stove, I
changed my plan, and instead of placing them between
the Guards' camp, thought it would be better to have
them in the centre of the Highland Brigade, as near as
possible to Sir Colin Campbell's headquarters, which
would enable him to watch the proceedings without
trouble. For this purpose, I went to his quarters, and
was told that the best time to see him was from eight till
nine in the morning at the latest. Next morning I was on
my way to the Scotch camp by seven o'clock. I saw Colonel Stirling, Sir Colin's private secretary, who informed

me that Sir Colin would be happy to receive me. My reception by that brave and illustrious general was highly gratifying to my feelings.

'Welcome, Monsieur Soyer!' exclaimed the general, as I entered his tent. He shook me by the hand, with a smile on his face which one could see came from the heart. The fine long beard which then adorned his visage could only be portrayed by a Rembrandt or a Titian. The amiable and fine qualities of that noble-hearted general, so well known to every Englishman, made me feel proud of being so cordially received by one the pride of his country.

'How are you, Monsieur Soyer?'

'Never better, general,' was my answer. 'I am happy to see you are enjoying good health.'

'Thank God, I am. Be seated, and tell me what I can do for you.'

'I shall esteem it a great favour, general, if you will allow me to place my new field stoves in your brigade, instead of on the esplanade. Your men have, unknown to me, commenced cooking with them; and as they already know how to use them, I should prefer leaving them in their hands.'

'Very well, Monsieur Soyer; select the spot, and Colonel Stirling will give you all the assistance you may require.'

'Thank you, general; but I must observe that this is only a trial, and they will be removed as soon as the commander-in-chief has seen them in use, and decided upon their merits.'

After taking some refreshment, kindly offered by the general, I went to Colonel Stirling, and informed him of the general's decision. He promised to have everything ready to commence operations the next morning.

The following day I was out very early at the Inkermann heights, with a numerous party, looking towards the Tchernaya Bridge. It was the 16th of August, the day of that memorable battle, which does not require a description on my part. From four till eight that morning I looked on, and saw the retreat of the Russians and the triumph of the French and Sardinians.

On my return, I had the pleasure of riding with Lord Rokeby, who was on his way to his quarters to give some important orders. I had a very interesting conversation with his lordship, who explained the plan of the battle – how it commenced and ended, with the probable loss on both sides. He had been up all night: reinforcements were pouring in from all directions of the Allied camps, with the cavalry, then commanded by General Scarlett, as another attack was expected. Near Lord Rokeby's quarters we met Colonel Seymour, who gave him a despatch, whereupon the former immediately left us. The colonel rode with me some distance, giving me more details respecting the engagement. He then remarked that I had not called the day before, according to promise. I told him that I had been detained later than I anticipated: I also mentioned my interview with Sir Colin Campbell. He said –

'You have done well, Monsieur Soyer; but of course I shall not be able to do so much for you, as I am in another brigade: however, I will do my utmost.' He then observed, 'I believe, though I was introduced to you the other day by General Simpson, you do not recollect me.'

'To be frank with you, colonel, I must acknowledge

that your face is very familiar, but I cannot recall where I had the pleasure of seeing you before.'

'You will remember me, when I tell you I have been many times in your kitchen at the Reform Club. Do you recollect me now?'

This explanation not having enlightened me, he continued –

'It was I – then Captain Seymour – who accompanied the Prince of Prussia, the Duke of Saxe-Coburg, the Grand Duke Michael, the Princess Clementia of France, and his Royal Highness Prince Albert, whose aide-de-camp I was for several years.'

It was not until he said this that I recalled the colonel's face, as he had been completely metamorphosed from the drawing-room dandy to a fierce and war-worn warrior. I was now much delighted to find so firm a supporter of my undertaking. I could not, however, account for the sudden change in his appearance since I had seen him at the Reform Club.

I went to see Colonel Stirling, though not expecting to find him or Sir Colin in the camp, when, by chance, he returned, having important business to transact. Upon seeing me, he said –

'Ah, Monsieur Soyer, you have selected a very glorious day for the commencement of your hostilities; but I regret I shall not be able to assist you, as we do not know how this affair will be decided.'

'You do not for a moment suppose, colonel, that I would intrude upon your valuable time on such an occasion? Having slept in camp, I only called *en passant*. Good-morning, colonel.'

'Good-day, Soyer. I would advise you to call tomorrow.'

Having given a look at my Highlanders' cooking, and tasted some coffee which they had prepared for breakfast according to my receipt, I retired, much pleased with their success.

I remained at the camp till nearly three in the afternoon. About one, a long train of mules made their appearance, bearing wounded French and Russian soldiers – the latter prisoners. About twenty were wounded; the rest followed the mournful procession. Assisted by a few of my men, I gave them some wine, brandy, porter, &c. – in fact, whatever we could get at the canteen – which seemed to afford them much relief. I of course treated the wounded Russians in the same manner as the French; though two refused to take anything, fearing poison.

Not doubting that many more would pass, as I had some provisions in a tent for the opening of my kitchens, I made some sago jelly, with wine, calfs'-foot jelly, &c., which unfortunately was not used, as the other prisoners went by a different road, though taken to the General Hospital at the French headquarters. Upon leaving, I ordered my men to be on the look out, and if any wounded or prisoners came by, to offer them some refreshment.

Just as I was going, I perceived a few mules approaching the Guards' camp. As they advanced, I and one of my men went towards some of the wounded with a basin of sago in hand, saying, this was a sort of half-way ambulance, where they might obtain all they might require. I was aware that some of the Russian prisoners in the first convoy would not accept any refreshment, for fear of being poisoned, of course not knowing better. The case of two poor French soldiers I cannot pass in silence. One had been severely wounded in the head, and was almost in a state of insensibility; the other had had his leg amputated on the field of battle. The first, after taking a few spoonfuls of the hot sago, asked for a drop of brandy, saying he felt faint. The conductor at first objected to this, but upon my asking him to take a glass with me and the patient, he agreed that it would do him no harm if it did him no good – adding, that very likely he would not survive the day. Having mixed it with water, he drank it, and thanked me warmly. The other was an officer. After giving him some wine-jelly, I conversed with him.

'How good this jelly is!' said he, in French; 'pray give me another spoonful or two, if you have it to spare.'

Having done this, he said that he suddenly felt very thirsty. This was, no doubt, owing to the loss of blood. I gave him some lemonade. He drank above a pint, and felt more composed, and proceeded to the hospital, near the English headquarters. I accompanied him, and he told me that his leg had just been amputated; and, with tears in his eyes, added, in a low voice, 'All I regret is, that my military career should have ended so soon. I am but thirty years of age, and have only been two months in the Crimea.'

'My dear friend,' I replied, to cheer him, 'many thousands have done less, and died; but you will survive, and be rewarded for your gallant service – you belong to a nation which can appreciate noble devotion.'

'Ah!' said he, 'you have done me a deal of good, no matter who you are; if my life is spared, I beg you will let me see or hear from you.'

Though he gave me his name, not having my pocket-book with me, I could not make a note of it. Some time after, I visited the hospital, in company with Dr. Wyatt of the Coldstream Guards. We learnt that the man who had been wounded in the head had died, but that the officer whose leg had been amputated had been sent home to France.

About six in the evening, I and my Zouave visited the field of battle. The sight was indeed a melancholy one. The French and Sardinians were busily engaged burying their dead, as well as those of the enemy, but were compelled to desist several times in consequence of the Russian cannonade from the heights.

Bornet, my Zouave, perceiving that the Russians were firing upon the Allies while burying their dead, got in such a towering passion, that I thought he would have gone alone and taken the Russian batteries. I had great difficulty in getting him home, for, as I have before said, the smell of gunpowder was to him like the scent of a rat to a terrier.

On arriving on board the *Baraguay d'Hilliers*, we learnt from the captain that he was to take his departure in a few days, at which I was very sorry, not having opened my kitchen, nor being as yet installed in the camp. I applied to the harbourmaster, who advised me to choose the *Edward*; as she was a transport and laden with hospital stores, she was likely to remain longest in harbour.

I was at this time busily engaged pitching my tents in

the camp. The opening of my kitchen was delayed in consequence of the troops being on duty at the Tchernaya. This lasted for about ten days, when it was rumoured that Sir Colin Campbell wished to remove his camp to Kamara, in order to be nearer the spot at which it was supposed the expected attack would take place. I therefore pitched my tent on the spot I had at first selected. The day for my opening ceremony was fixed upon by General Simpson; and my friend Colonel Seymour very kindly assisted me in many ways, and even wrote letters of invitation to the colonels and officers of the different regiments. I was anxious for them to give their approval or non-approval of the method. Two days before, Colonel Seymour and myself had settled everything to our satisfaction, and wishing to make a kind of *fête champêtre* of the opening day, we applied at proper quarters for a band of music, which was granted.

My opening day was the one fixed upon for the distribution of the Order of the Bath. In parting from the colonel, he observed, 'Well, Monsieur Soyer, I think we shall make a good thing of this, unless something happens to me in the trenches to-night. I am just going there.'

These words were said in as light-hearted a manner as though he was going to a ball, and passed from my mind as quickly. The gallant colonel was then going perhaps for the hundredth time to his dangerous and uncertain duty.

I returned to Balaklava for the last time previous to taking up my permanent residence at the camp. I had settled all to my entire satisfaction. With Sir George Maclean, the

Commissary-General, I had arranged respecting the quantity of rations required for a certain number of men; with Mr. Fitzgerald, the Deputy Purveyor-in-chief, for the fresh meat; and with the butcher for a supply of four ox-heads and six ox-feet, out of the number he daily buried. I placed all my people in their different stations according to merit and qualification. I obtained from Major Mackenzie, through the kindness of Sir Thomas Eyre, the Ordnance Master, some wood and four carpenters to put up some tables and a few benches, and ordered from Messrs. Crockford, at Donnybrook, a certain quantity of wines and refreshments worthy of the illustrious guests I was about to receive.

Opening of Soyer's field kitchen before Sebastopol

My Great Field Day

My gallant master of the ceremonies, Colonel Seymour, had kindly taken the most important part of my duty off my hands, by inviting all the heads of the military and medical authorities, with a great number of whom, in consequence of my short stay in the Crimea, I was not yet, or, at least, only partially acquainted. I had now removed to the *Edward*, and also left her, but still kept, if not a *pied à terre* (as we say in French), at least a *pied sur mer*, for myself and people, in case I should require to go to Balaklava and stay there for the night.

This was on the 26th of August, 1855 – the 27th was to be the opening day. All my people had left for the camp, with arms and baggage. I was certain of success and without the slightest anxiety. On arriving at my field of operations, I learnt, to my deep sorrow, that my right hand, Colonel Seymour, had, during the night, been dangerously wounded in the trenches. I immediately went to his quarters to ascertain the nature of his wound. His servant told me, that for the present no one could tell; he had been struck by the splinter of a shell at the back of the neck, the wound was not so bad as had been at first anticipated. His servant announced me, and although very weak, the colonel begged I would enter his tent. He was lying upon the ground upon a blanket, covered with another, and his military cloak over that.

His head was bandaged with a turban of white linen stained with blood. His first words were, 'Monsieur Soyer, you see what has happened at last. I much regret it, as I shall not be able to perform my promise to you respecting your opening.'

'Never mind, colonel; don't let us talk about that subject now, but about yourself.'

'Well,' he replied, 'the doctor has just been, and says that the wound is not mortal, nor even so dangerous as he at first anticipated.'

'Colonel, you want repose, so I will retire.'

'There is no occasion for that, Monsieur Soyer; I feel strong again. When I was struck, I did not feel the wound, and fell immediately, remaining for some time insensible, the wound, as the doctor says, having acted upon the brain.'

'Don't exert yourself, my dear colonel, by talking. Thank God it is no worse. I will go and send you some lemonade. I have asked the doctor what was best for you, and am happy to say I have some ice.'

'Many thanks for your kind attention, Monsieur Soyer.'

I then retired. Upon reaching my kitchen, I found that no one had yet arrived. The four carpenters had left me in the lurch, having run away in the night, and abandoned their work, after stealing all they could from the tents. Mr. Doyne, the chief of the Army Works Corps, kindly supplied me with workmen, and offered to lend me, for a few days, as many tents as I required. As the weather was then intensely hot, I accepted his offer, and requested the loan of a large marquee, under which a couple of hundred people could stand. Captain Gordon lent me two smaller ones, and by the evening they were pitched, and my provisions had all arrived, and my people were at their posts.

I much regretted that many persons of distinction were not invited, in consequence of the unfortunate accident to Colonel Seymour, which happened before he had sent out all the invitations. At all events, the day, though fixed at hazard, turned out extremely well adapted for the reception of a large party.

Early in the morning the camp seemed full of life and gaiety. Mounted officers in full uniform might be seen rushing about in all directions; bands were playing, regiments filing past, and everything bearing the appearance of a great festival. I set cheerfully to work, and, in spite of difficulties which can only be understood by those who have been in the Crimea, I succeeded in getting all in tolerably good order for my great martial banquet *al fresco*. I made several messes with the soldiers' rations, and at the same expense, though I had introduced sauce and ingredients which could easily be added to the army stores without increasing the cost, thus making a nice variation in the meals, so important to the health of a large body of men like the army or navy, to the latter of which it is as easily applicable as the former.

The bill of fare consisted of plain boiled salt beef; ditto, with dumplings; plain boiled salt pork; ditto, with peas-pudding; stewed salt pork and beef, with rice; French pot-au-feu; stewed fresh beef, with potatoes; mutton, ditto, with haricot beans; ox-cheek and ox-feet soups; Scotch mutton-broth; common curry, made with fresh and salt beef. (See receipts in Addenda.)

By three o'clock my guests began to arrive. The stoves were in the open air, placed in a semicircle, and, though in a state of ebullition, no one could perceive that any cooking was going on, except on raising the lids. A material point I had in view was that no fire should be seen when used in the trenches. A common table, made of a few boards, and garnished with soldiers' tin plates, iron forks and spoons, composed my open-air dining-room.

About four o'clock my reception commenced. Lord Rokeby, accompanied by several French officers in full dress, was the first to honour me with a visit. This gave me an opportunity of fully explaining to him and his friends the plan and construction of the apparatus, as well as its simplicity, cleanliness, and great economy in the consumption of fuel. At the same time, I showed with what ease and certainty the men could regulate the heat and prepare the new receipts – which will be found at the end of this work.

I must also observe, for the information of those who only saw them upon that occasion, that the stoves, having been made for the General Hospital, were too large and heavy for campaigning. That I might lose no time in making my trial before the authorities, I used them upon that occasion, as the process was the same as regards cooking in those as in the smaller ones. The sole difference was in the size, as it was understood that two would cook for a company of one hundred and twenty men, and might be carried by one mule while on march, with sufficient dry wood inside for the next day's cooking.

This was of the utmost importance, in order to ensure the regularity of the soldier's meal, which ought always to be ready at the minute fixed by the rules of the service.

Thus I had surmounted every difficulty by the invention of this apparatus. In addition to its simplicity and economy, it had the merit of making cooks of soldiers, of which they had previously neither the inclination nor the chance. Smaller stoves on the same principle were also to be provided for picket and outpost duty, as first suggested to me by Lord Raglan. After giving the foregoing information to my illustrious visitors, we passed to the grand process of tasting the various messes. They all gave perfect satisfaction.

By this time several hundred visitors had made their appearance, and gay and animated was the scene. All present were in the same costume as that in which they appeared at the grand chivalric ceremony which had taken place at headquarters – the installation of the Order of the Bath. I was also highly favoured, I may say, by the presence of a charming group of the fair sex, about ten in number, escorted by their cavaliers. After taking some refreshment under the monster tent, they came to add their charms to the martial banquet, and taste with gusto the rough food of the brave. I had nothing out of doors to offer their delicate palates but the soldiers' rations, transmogrified in various ways. My task now became extremely difficult. The crowd was so great, that my batteries were quite taken by storm (*de cuisine*, of course). Refreshments of all kinds were distributed pretty freely throughout the day. The band in attendance was ordered to play, and struck up 'Partant pour la Syrie.' All were immediately on the *qui vive*, when Captain Colville galloped up to me, and said –

'General Simpson has sent me to inform you that General Pelissier and himself will be here in a few minutes.'

A gorgeous cavalcade was soon seen in the distance. It consisted of the Allied Generals and staff, and a numerous suite. General Pelissier alighted from his carriage, and joined General Simpson. I went and met the distinguished visitors, who had come from headquarters after the ceremony of the distribution of the Order of the Bath by Lord Stratford de Redcliffe.

Upon the arrival of the generals, the band continued playing 'Partant pour la Syrie.' The cannon of Sebastopol appeared to redouble its roar – so much so, that General Pelissier, with a smile, called General Simpson's attention to the fact: added to which, the hundreds of uniforms, cocked hats and feathers – French, English, and Sardinian – gave full effect to the lively scene.

In course of conversation, General Simpson said, 'Monsieur Soyer, – Lord Stratford de Redcliffe, in reply to your letter, sends his compliments, and regrets he shall not be able to attend your opening, as he must be on board the *Caradoc*, now lying in Kamiesch Bay, by five o'clock, on his way to Constantinople.'

I thanked General Simpson for his kindness in troubling himself about the message, and the review of my culinary camp, which upon this occasion was rather extensive, commenced. It comprised four bell-tents, one marquee, and a large square tent, capable of holding more than two hundred persons. A luncheon *al fresco* was served in the camp, and four of my cooks attended upon the guests. The tops of the tents were surmounted with flags and garlands of evergreens composed of vine-leaves; the same were also attached to the posts which supported the rope forming the limits of the enclosure, giving to the whole a martial and lively appearance. The weather was so fine that everyone preferred remaining in the open air.

Generals Pelissier and Simpson proceeded to taste the various articles of food. The *pot-au-feu*, or beef-soup, was prepared partly from ox-heads, which were usually buried, instead of being used as food for the soldiers, no doubt in consequence of the difficulty of cleaning them.

General Pelissier tasted several samples of the pot-au-feu, and, addressing General Barnard, declared that he felt as interested in this unexpected exhibition as in the ceremony of the morning. The witty General Barnard replied, 'Your excellency must agree with me that this day has been remarkably well spent: we devoted the morning to the *cordon rouge*, and the afternoon to the *cordon bleu*.' General Pelissier much enjoyed the *bon mot*, and repeated it to the officers of his staff, thus creating great hilarity amongst them.

I requested many of my visitors to taste the different preparations, and, much to my satisfaction, I believe almost all of them did so, and expressed their approbation of them. After pointing out the merits of the stoves to the commanders-in-chief, I conducted them to the spot where the Scotch Division formerly cooked their rations in the old tin camp-kettles. On our way, I observed to General Pelissier that I had visited the French camp-kitchens, and found their marmites superior to the English. The soup made by the French soldiers, I said, was very good. At this the General seemed much pleased.

The space required for three or four regiments extended about three hundred and fifty feet in length. A rough wall of loose stones had been erected by the men to form a screen, which when the regiment moved was, of course, left behind. The furnaces were also constructed of loose stones, held together by iron hoops; upon these the tin cans were placed and the rations cooked. By this plan an immense quantity of wood was inevitably wasted, and the fires were sometimes extinguished by the heavy rains. My stoves completely obviated all those previously insurmountable difficulties.

Having listened to this explanation, the commanders-in-chief admitted the beneficial results and advantages of the stoves. However, General Simpson observed that I, of course, applied the contrast to my advantage; but also said, it was nothing but fair, and I was perfectly justified in so doing. In the first place, my stoves occupied but little room, and cooked much better than those formerly in use.

The Allied Generals remained with me above an hour. This gave me an excellent opportunity of conversing with General Pelissier, who minutely described camp life in Algeria, after which the General and Staff retired. As it was then nearly seven o'clock, a great number of officers followed. No less than eight hundred or a thousand persons of distinction visited the kitchens during the day: many were not invited, in consequence of the unfortunate accident to Colonel Seymour. About nine all was over, and the band played 'God save the Queen.'

Nothing could have succeeded better than this opening,

a drawing of which appeared in the *Illustrated News* of September 22nd, 1855.

General Pelissier's Letter

J'ai eu le plasir, le vingt-sept Août, 1855, de visiter l'établissement culinaire de Monsieur Soyer, et j'ai été bien satisfait de ce que j'y ai vu; j'ai été frappé surtout de l'économie de temps et de chauffage apporté dans l'alimentation des troupes. Les chaudières paraissent bien entendues; j'ai tout goûté, et à tout, je le reconnais, j'ai trouvé un goût excellent et très-appétissant.*

General A. Pelissier.

General Simpson's Letter.

Camp before Sebastopol, 31st August, 1855.
I had much pleasure in visiting Monsieur Soyer's field-kitchen last Monday, the 27th instant. I there saw several excellent soups made from ration meat, compressed vegetables, and other things within reach of the soldier's means, and cooked with very little fuel. I consider Monsieur Soyer is taking great pains in devoting his time and great talents to the good of our military service, especially in the field, and I wish him every possible success and honourable reward.

James Simpson,
General Commanding.

* On the 27th of August, 1855, I had the pleasure of visiting Mr Soyer's culinary establishment and I was well satisfied with what I saw there. I was particularly struck with the saving of time and fuel which has been made in catering for the troops. The stores appear well arranged. I tasted everything and found it all most appetising.

WAR OFFICE, *6th August,* 1855.

*SIR, – I am directed to acknowledge the receipt, on the 2nd
ultimo, of your report upon the culinary department of the
hospitals in the East; and, in returning the thanks of the
Secretary-at-War, to acquaint you, that he recognises, with
the greatest satisfaction, the exertions you have made and
are still making for the benefit of the army in the field, and
also of the sick and wounded in the several hospitals.*

I am, Sir, your obedient servant,

M. Soyer, Scutari.   FRED. J. PRESCOTT.

About the 5th of September, I was at headquarters,
when who should walk in but Sir Edmund Lyons! I had
not the pleasure of seeing him before, and I took this
opportunity of introducing myself, and informing the
Commander of the British Fleet in the Black Sea that I was
very anxious to pay my respectful compliments to him.

Upon this, Sir Edmund Lyons, with the kindest feel-
ing, at once offered me his hand, saying, 'Monsieur
Soyer, I assure you I am delighted to make your acquaintance. You are doing much good for our brave soldiers;
but you must not forget our worthy sailors. Come and
see us on board the *Albert*; you will be well received and
quite welcome. I have heard much about your field-
kitchens, and it was only the other day I was reading a
very important complimentary letter which General
Pelissier had written in their favour.'

'He did me that honour, admiral, and he seemed
highly gratified.'

'I can assure you he was, Monsieur Soyer, for I heard
him say so.'

A few days after the grand opening ceremony, a meeting took place, by order of the Minister-at-War and General Simpson, to consider the possibility of supplying a pint of hot soup to the men in the trenches during the winter. The meeting was held at Lord Rokeby's headquarters, on the 3rd or 4th of September. I was ordered to be present. On my way there I had the pleasure of meeting General Barnard, who in his humorous manner addressed me thus: –

'Hallo, General Soyer! I'm not so much behind as I thought; for you are only just going to the general meeting, or the meeting of generals.'

'You are right, general,' I replied. 'Thank you for the noble title you have bestowed upon me, and at the seat of war too.'

'The fact is, I understood the meeting was to be held at headquarters, and went half-way there, when I met some officers who told me it was to be at Lord Rokeby's. But they cannot proceed without you, general. Never mind, Soyer, we are only a few minutes behind time.'

When we arrived, the Board was sitting. Sir Colin Campbell had sent a message, stating that some important duties would prevent his attendance. The proceedings then commenced, and the order was read by General Bentinck; which, as far as I can recollect, was worded thus: –

Lord Panmure, the Minister-at-War, anxious for the comfort of the troops in the Crimea, is desirous that, if possible, every man in the trenches should be supplied with a basin of hot soup during the winter nights; the allowance of rum to be, in consequence, either diminished or entirely withheld. His lordship believing Monsieur Soyer to be still in the Crimea, requests the Board to inquire of him if such would be practicable.

I at once replied that it could be done, and without difficulty, for any number of men, by the application of my field stoves. This answer met with the general approbation of the assembled Board. I next remarked that the stoves might be placed in the trenches, even in front of the enemy, as not a spark of fire could be seen either by day or night while they were in use. This point having been satisfactorily settled, the question of taking away or reducing the quantity of rum was seriously debated. General Eyre was of opinion that the men would not like to part with any portion of their rum. Generals Bentinck, Rokeby, &c., were in favour of giving the soup as an addition, and allowing the rum to be issued as usual. It struck me that by giving only half a gill of rum the other half would almost entirely cover the expense of the soup, if economically managed. I also proposed another plan, which was to give less rum and less than a pint of soup, which was discussed.

When the inquiry was over, I said – 'Gentlemen, I shall feel obliged if you will favour me with a visit to my field kitchen. I have made several experiments in diets for you to taste, and if you approve of them, have no doubt when you know the cost, you will be able to settle the question of supplying soup in the trenches with more certainty.'

All present agreed, excepting General Eyre, who

was of opinion that what he as a soldier had for so many years found answer for the men, would answer now; nor did he see why the soldiers should live better than himself. 'I should be very happy,' said he, 'to improve the daily food of the troops, but do not like anything to be overdone. I like judicious discipline in all things.'

Though I must frankly admit I was anything but enchanted with the general's way of thinking at first, I could not but admire the latter part of his argument, which was as sincere as it was severe.

Several debates took place upon the subject, and, after a little persuasion, I induced them all to come, and taste the samples I had prepared for their inspection. I proudly led my very select cavalcade towards my batteries, which upon that occasion were in charge of the troops. I had only given the written receipts for them to act upon, and charged a serjeant to watch over them, and see that the proportions in the receipts were properly attended to. An infallible plan of ensuring success at all times is to appoint a man of superior grade as overlooker. One to each regiment would be sufficient.

Upon our arrival we found everything in perfect order: the stoves were clean, the contents properly cooked, and the consumption of fuel four hundred per cent. less than in the usual way. Only five different messes were prepared upon this occasion – viz., ox-head soup, stewed fresh beef, Scotch hodge-podge of mutton, salt pork and beef with dumplings. Everything was done to perfection. After carefully explaining the process to Generals Eyre and Bentinck, who were not present on the great opening day, we sat down to test the quality of the articles. A sumptuous lunch was displayed from the soldiers' rations – always excepting the ox-heads, which I had obtained from the butcher, as usual, on the eve of their funeral. With these I made an excellent *pot-au-feu*, enough for fifty men. Lord Rokeby was so highly delighted with it, that he recommended it to all, and requested me to give this receipt, as well as that for stewed beef, to his cook – for which see Addenda.

A goblet of Marsala wine, with a lump of ice, terminated this martial collation under a burning sun, and amid the everlasting roar of the bombardment of the besieged city. The guests retired, quite satisfied. Even General Eyre, though still adhering to his opinion that it was too good for soldiers, and would make them lazy, said, 'Soldiers do not require such good messes as those while campaigning.' At which remark the gentlemen present could not refrain from laughing.

'Well, general,' said I, 'your plan has been tried, and, as you perceive, has not answered. I was therefore obliged to introduce a simpler style, by which soldiers might cook with pleasure and less difficulty, and, having once learnt, always will cook properly, and with less trouble. You must also observe, general, that it is with the same rations as before. And is it not better to make a few good cooks out of an army than to have an army of bad cooks?'

By this time the general was on his charger. He said, 'We are both right. For my part, I mean what I say: you will improve the cook, but spoil the soldier.'

I then thanked them for their gracious condescension,

and they started for their several divisions, promising to let me know their final decision.

Amongst the military authorities who visited me that day were General Scarlett and staff, Colonel St. George, Colonel Handcock and lady, a very charming person, and extremely merry. She observed, when I presented her with some champagne and ice in a large tin goblet, as she sat upon her horse, 'Upon my word, Monsieur Soyer, champagne is better in tin cups in the Crimea than in crystal goblets in England.'

'I am glad you like it, madam. Shall I offer you another?'

'No, I thank you.'

'Madam would like to taste some of the men's rations,' said Colonel Handcock.

'Would you, madam?'

'Many thanks, Monsieur Soyer. I think not, after the champagne.'

After paying a visit to my abode, my guests departed.

A few days afterwards, I heard that that poor creature was plunged in the deepest sorrow. Upon making a chance visit, I could not believe her to be the same person; the bloom of life appeared to have suddenly deserted her laughing cheeks, which wore a cadaverous hue. Such was the effect sorrow soon produced on the appearance of one usually so animated and full of mirth.

As I noticed that the men daily threw the fat away from their salt beef and pork, the last of which is of first-rate quality, I proposed to Colonel Daniell, of the Coldstream Guards, to make his men cook for his regiment, which was agreed upon. He always took great interest in the welfare of his soldiers and in my culinary proceedings, and I had the honour of being acquainted with him for some years as a subscriber to benevolent institutions, and in particular to soup-kitchens for the poor. The next day the rations were brought in; the salt beef and pork were cooked, and a few dumplings added, as an innovation. The wood was weighed, and twenty-seven pounds were sufficient to cook the rations for the whole regiment. The meat was done to perfection, and without trouble. I begged that the sixteen cooks daily employed for the regiment might be present. Two would have done, or even one, as the water and provisions were brought by a fatigue party, therefore fifteen men might have been spared; and only forty-seven pounds of wood were used, instead of one thousand seven hundred and sixty. When the meat was cooked, we skimmed off forty-two pounds of fat as white as snow, and not black, as was the case when cooked in the small canteen-pans with little water. This spoilt the fat, which might be used in lieu of butter on bread or biscuit. To do this properly, soak the biscuits in water for about ten minutes; take them out, let them dry a little; put some fat in the pan; when hot, fry them as you would a piece of bacon: a few minutes will do them. When crisp, season with salt and pepper, if handy. They make an excellent article of food.

For this saving and improvement, Colonel Daniell, whom I will back for discipline and straightforwardness of opinion against anyone in the army, gave me the following letter: –

COLDSTREAM GUARDS' CAMP, BEFORE
SEBASTOPOL, *Sept.*, 1855.

*I have this day attended Monsieur Soyer's course of
instruction to the cooks of my battalion, and have tasted the
messes cooked and served to the men, consisting of salt pork
and beef. The mode in which the salt is extracted and the
meat rendered comparatively tender by the apparatus used,
the facility with which the grease is taken off and rendered
serviceable for other purposes, is admirable; and I consider
the arrangements relative to the small consumption of
wood, and the simplicity with which the cooking is
conducted, will, if adopted, tend much to the health,
comfort, and well-being of the soldier.*

*The present size of the 'chaudrières' being objectionable,
I am glad to hear from Monsieur Soyer that he is about to
procure some of a less size. The fuel consumed today for
cooking the messes of eight companies was hardly more
than on ordinary occasions is consumed by one company;
and from four hundred and twenty rations of salt pork and
beef forty-eight pounds of excellent lard was procured,
which usually is wasted. These facts alone render Monsieur
Soyer's plan at once economical and desirable, and I have
great pleasure in testifying my appreciation of the manner
with which he conveys instruction to the men, in saying
how highly I approve of his recipes and arrangements for
carrying out his scheme of camp cookery.*

(Signed) H. J. DANIELL,
*Col. and Capt. in Command, First Battalion
Coldstream Guards.*

The regiments being at that time greatly reduced,

were only 428 strong, therefore the weight of meat, at one pound per man, was 428 pounds, from which 42 pounds of excellent fat were obtained, much preferable for cooking purposes to the rancid butter sold in the canteens at a very high price. As I was anxious to form a perfect regimental kitchen, I proposed to Colonel Daniell to fit up one for his regiment. His men were already well acquainted with the use of the field stoves; and it would serve as a model for all. Colonel Daniell agreed, and in less than an hour the stoves were removed to the camp,

Soyer's field stove

where they remained by sanction of the General-in-Chief till the end of the war.

At this time I went to headquarters, and urged the necessity of telegraphing an order for four hundred small field stoves, which order had been agreed upon in case my plan succeeded and was adopted by the authorities. I also had several interviews with General Airey upon the subject. This number was sufficient for the supply of the whole of the army then in the Crimea. As there was so much business at headquarters in consequence of the anticipated attack upon Sebastopol, the order was postponed for a few days.

Soyer Très Heureux

The Author, after his laborious campaign, in bidding adieu to his readers, does not intend to remain *Soyer tranquille*, as he is most anxious, after having chronicled his culinary reminiscences of the late war, to put his views into action by simple practice; and as he had no other object in writing this book, he sincerely hopes it may be the means of causing a lasting amelioration in the cooking for both army and navy, and all public institutions. Such a result to his labours, after his long culinary experience, would make the author happy indeed, and he would for the future be found as traced below.

Soyer très heureux

Soyer's Hospital Diets
As introduced by him with the concurrence of the leading medical gentlemen of the British military hospitals in the East

The importance attaching to weights and measures in the accompanying receipts is fully recognised; it is therefore necessary that regimental as well as civil hospitals should be supplied with scales, and with measures for liquids.

NO. 1 – SEMI-STEWED MUTTON AND BARLEY. SOUP FOR 100 MEN.

Put in a convenient-sized caldron 130 pints of cold water, 70lbs. of meat, or about that quantity, 12lbs. of plain mixed vegetables (the best that can be obtained), 9lbs. of barley, 1lb. 7oz. of salt, 1lb. 4oz. of flour, 1lb. 4oz. of sugar, 1oz. of pepper. Put all the ingredients into the pan at once, except the flour; set it on the fire, and when beginning to boil, diminish the heat, and simmer gently for two hours and a half; take the joints of meat out, and keep them warm in the orderly's pan; add to the soup your flour, which you have mixed with enough water to form a light batter; stir well together with a large spoon; boil another half-hour, skim off the fat, and serve the soup and meat separate. The meat may be put back into the soup for a few minutes to warm again prior to serving. The soup should be stirred now and then while making, to prevent burning or sticking to the bottom of the caldron.

The joints are cooked whole, and afterwards cut up in different messes; being cooked this way, in a rather thick stock, the meat becomes more nutritous.

Note. – The word 'about' is applied to the half and full diet, which varies the weight of the meat; but ½lb. of mutton will always make a pint of good soup: 3lbs. of mixed preserved vegetables must be used when fresh are not to be obtained, and put in one hour and a half prior to serving, instead of at first; they will then show better in the soup, and still be well done.

All the following receipts may be increased to large quantities, but by all means closely follow the weight and measure.

NO. 12 – CALF'S-FOOT JELLY.

Put in a proper sized stewpan 2¼oz. of calf's-foot gelatine, 4oz. of white sugar, 4 whites of eggs and shells, the peel of a lemon, the juice of three middle-sized lemons, half a pint of Marsala wine; beat all well together with the egg beater for a few minutes, then add 4½ pints of cold water; set it on a slow fire, and keep whipping it till boiling. Set it on the corner of the stove, partly covered with the lid, upon which you place a few pieces of burning charcoal; let it simmer gently for ten minutes, and strain it through a jelly-bag. It is then ready to put in the ice or some cool place. Sherry will do if Marsala is not at hand.

For orange jelly use only 1 lemon and 2 oranges. Any delicate flavour may be introduced.

Note. – I find that the preparation now manufactured by Messrs. Crosse and Blackwell, of Soho Square, London, is preferable to any other, being also cheaper than boiling calfs' feet on purpose, which takes a very long time, and is more difficult to make. This preparation will keep as long as isinglass, to prove which I am induced at the same time to give the following receipt, when the other cannot be procured. Ox-feet or cow-heel may be used instead of calfs'-feet, only requiring an hour more simmering. In summer ice must be used to set the jelly.

JELLY STOCK.

Made from calf's-feet, requires to be made the day previous to being used, requiring to be very hard to extract the fat. Take two calf's-feet, cut them up, and boil in three quarts of water; as soon as it boils remove it to the corner of the fire, and simmer for five hours, keeping it skimmed, pass through a hair sieve into a basin, and let it remain until quite hard, then remove the oil and fat, and wipe the top dry. Place in a stew-pan half a pint of water, one of sherry, half a pound of lump sugar, the juice of four lemons, the rinds of two, and the whites and shells of five eggs; whisk until the sugar is melted, then add the jelly, place it on the fire, and whisk until boiling, pass it through a jelly-bag, pouring that back again which comes through first until quite clear; it is then ready for use, by putting it in moulds or glasses. Vary the flavour according to fancy.

NO. 13 – SAGO JELLY.

Put into a pan 3oz. of sago, 1½oz. of sugar, half a lemon-peel cut very thin, ¼ teaspoonful of ground cinnamon, or a small stick of the same; put to it 3 pints of water and a little salt; boil ten minutes, or rather longer, stirring continually, until rather thick, then add a little port, sherry, or Marsala wine; mix well, and serve hot or cold.

NO. 15 – THICK ARROWROOT PANADA.

Put in a pan 5oz. of arrowroot, 2½oz. of white sugar, the peel of half a lemon, a quarter of a teaspoonful of salt, 4 pints of water; mix all well, set on the fire, boil for ten minutes; it is then ready. The juice of a lemon is an improvement; a gill of wine may also be introduced, and ½oz. of calf's-foot gelatine previously dissolved in water will be strengthening. Milk, however, is preferable, if at hand.

NO. 17 – RICE WATER

Put 7 pints of water to boil, add to it 2 ounces of rice washed, 2oz. of sugar, the peel of two-thirds of a lemon; boil gently for three-quarters of an hour; it will reduce to 5 pints; strain through a colander; it is then ready.

The rice may be left in the beverage or made into a pudding, or by the addition of a little sugar or jam, will be found very good for either children or invalids.

NO. 18 – BARLEY WATER

Put in a saucepan 7 pints of water, 2oz. of barley, which stir now and then while boiling; add 2oz. of white sugar, the rind of half a lemon, thinly peeled; let it boil gently for about two hours, without covering it; pass it through a sieve or colander; it is then ready. The barley and lemon may be left in it.

NO. 19 – SOYER'S PLAIN LEMONADE

Thinly peel the third part of a lemon, which put into a basin with 2 tablespoonfuls of sugar; roll the lemon with your hand upon the table to soften it; cut it into two, lengthwise, squeeze the juice over the peel, &c., stir round for a minute with a spoon to form a sort of syrup; pour over a pint of water, mix well, and remove the pips; it is then ready for use. If a very large lemon, and full of juice, and very fresh, you may make a pint and a half to a quart, adding sugar and peel in proportion to the increase of water. The juice only of the lemon and sugar will make lemonade, but will then be deprived of the aroma which the rind contains, the said rind being generally thrown away.

NO. 20 – SEMI-CITRIC LEMONADE.
RECEIPT FOR FIFTY PINTS

Put 1oz. of citric acid to dissolve in a pint of water; peel 20 lemons thinly, and put the peel in a large vessel, with 3lbs. 2oz. of white sugar well broken; roll each lemon on the table to soften it, which will facilitate the extraction of the juice; cut them into two, and press out the juice into a colander or sieve, over the peel and sugar, then pour half a pint of water through the colander, so as to leave no juice remaining; triturate the sugar, juice and peel together for a minute or two with a spoon, so as to form a sort of syrup, and extract the aroma from the peel and the dissolved citric acid; mix all well together, pour on 50 pints of cold water, stir well together; it is then ready. A little ice in summer is a great addition.

Observation. – The following Lemonade, which has been submitted to eminent Doctors at Scutari, has been approved of, and can be made for either the Hospitals or the Camp, and will be found to answer equally for domestic consumption, if lemons are not to be obtained.

NO. 21 – SOYER'S CHEAP CRIMEAN LEMONADE

Put into a basin 2 tablespoonfuls of white or brown sugar, ½ a tablespoonful of lime juice, mix well together for one minute, add 1 pint of water, and the beverage is ready. A drop of rum will make a good variation, as lime juice and rum are daily issued to the soldiers.

NO. 23 – CHEAP PLAIN RICE PUDDING, FOR CAMPAIGNING,

In which no eggs or milk are required: important in the Crimea or the field.

Put on the fire, in a moderate-sized saucepan, 12 pints of water; when boiling, add to it 1lb. of rice or 16 table-spoonfuls, 4oz. of brown sugar or 4 tablespoonfuls, 1 large teaspoonful of salt, and the rind of a lemon thinly peeled; boil gently for half an hour, then strain all the water from the rice, keeping it as dry as possible.

The rice-water is then ready for drinking, either warm or cold. The juice of a lemon may be introduced, which will make it more palatable and refreshing.

THE PUDDING

Add to the rice 3oz. of sugar, 4 tablespoonfuls of flour, half a teaspoonful of pounded cinnamon; stir it on the fire carefully for five or ten minutes; put it in a tin or a pie-dish, and bake. By boiling the rice a quarter of an hour longer, it will be very good to eat without baking. Cinnamon may be omitted.

NO. 24 – BREAD AND BUTTER PUDDING.

Butter a tart-dish well, and sprinkle some currants all round it, then lay in a few slices of bread and butter; boil one pint of milk, pour it on two eggs well whipped, and then on the bread and butter; bake it in a hot oven for half an hour. Currants may be omitted.

NO. 25 – BREAD PUDDING.

Boil one pint of milk, with a piece of cinnamon and lemon peel; pour it on two ounces of bread-crumbs;

then add two eggs, half an ounce of currants, and a little sugar: steam it in a buttered mould for one hour.

NO. 28 – STEWED MACARONI.

Put in a stewpan 2 quarts of water, half a tablespoonful of salt, 2oz. of butter; set on the fire; when boiling, add 1lb. of macaroni, broken up rather small; when boiled very soft, throw off the water; mix well into the macaroni a tablespoonful of flour, add enough milk to make it of the consistency of thin melted butter; boil gently twenty minutes; add in a tablespoonful of either brown or white sugar, or honey, and serve.

A little cinnamon, nutmeg, lemon peel, or orange-flower water may be introduced to impart a flavour; stir quick. A gill of milk or cream may now be thrown in three minutes before serving. Nothing can be more light and nutritious than macaroni done this way. If no milk, use water.

NO. 29 – MACARONI PUDDING.

Put 2 pints of water to boil, add to it 2oz. of macaroni, broken in small pieces; boil till tender, drain off the water and add half a tablespoonful of flour, 2oz. of white sugar, a quarter of a pint of milk, and boil together for ten minutes; beat an egg up, pour it to the other ingredients, a nut of butter; mix well and bake, or steam. It can be served plain, and may be flavoured with either cinnamon, lemon, or other essences, as orange-flower water, vanilla, &c.

NO. 35 – FRENCH HERB BROTH.

This is a very favourite beverage in France, as well with people in health as with invalids, especially in spring, when the herbs are young and green.

Put a quart of water to boil, having previously prepared about 40 leaves of sorrel, a cabbage lettuce, and 10 sprigs of chervil, the whole well washed; when the water is boiling, throw in the herbs, with the addition of a teaspoonful of salt, and ½oz. of fresh butter; cover the saucepan close, and let simmer a few minutes, then strain it through a sieve or colander.

This is to be drunk cold, especially in the spring of the year, after the change from winter. I generally drink about a quart per day for a week at that time; but if for sick people it must be made less strong of herbs, and taken a little warm.

To prove that it is wholesome, we have only to refer to the instinct which teaches dogs to eat grass at that season of the year. I do not pretend to say that it would suit persons in every malady, because the doctors are to decide upon the food and beverage of their patients, and study its changes as well as change their medicines; but I repeat that this is most useful and refreshing for the blood.

NO. 37 – TOAST-AND-WATER.

Cut a piece of crusty bread, about a ¼lb. in weight, place it upon a toasting-fork, and hold it about six inches from the fire; turn it often, and keep moving it gently until of a light yellow colour, then place it nearer the fire, and when of a good brown chocolate colour, put it in a jug and pour over 3 pints of boiling water; cover the jug until cold, then strain it into a clean jug, and it is ready for use. Never leave the toast in it, for in summer it would cause fermentation in a short time. I would almost venture to say that such toast-and-water as I have described, though so very simple, is the only way toast-water should be made, and that it would keep good a considerable time in bottles.

Baked Apple Toast-and-Water. – A piece of apple, slowly toasted till it gets quite black, and added to the above, makes a very nice and refreshing drink for invalids.

Apple Rice Water. – Half a pound of rice, boiled in the above until in pulp, passed through a colander, and drunk when cold.

All kinds of fruit may be done the same way.

Figs and French plums are excellent; also raisins.

A little ginger, if approved of, may be used.

Apple Barley Water. – A quarter of a pound of pearl barley instead of toast added to the above, and boiled for one hour, is also a very nice drink.

Citronade. – Put a gallon of water on to boil, cut up one pound of apples, each one into quarters, two lemons in thin slices, put them in the water, and boil them until they can be pulped, pass the liquor through a colander, boil it up again with half a pound of brown sugar, skim, and bottle for use, taking care not to cork the bottle, and keep it in a cool place.

For Spring Drink. – Rhubarb, in the same quantities, and done in the same way as apples, adding more sugar, is very cooling.

Also green gooseberries.

For Summer Drink. – One pound of red currants, bruised with some raspberry, half a pound of sugar added to a gallon of cold water, well stirred, and allowed to settle. The juice of a lemon.

Mulberry. – The same, adding a little lemon-peel.

A little cream of tartar or citric acid added to these renders them more cooling in summer and spring.

Plain Lemonade. – Cut in very thin slices three lemons, put them in a basin, add half a pound of sugar, either white or brown; bruise all together, add a gallon of water, and stir well. It is then ready.

French Plum Water. – Boil 3 pints of water; add in 6 or 8 dried plums previously split, 2 or 3 slices of lemon, a spoonful of honey or sugar; boil half an hour, and serve.

For *Fig, Date, and Raisin Water*, proceed as above, adding the juice of half a lemon to any of the above. If for fig water, use 6 figs.

Any quantity of the above fruits may be used with advantage in rice, barley, or arrowroot water.

Soyer's Field and Barrack Cookery for the Army

N.B. – These receipts are also applicable for barracks, in camp, or while on the march, by the use of Soyer's New Field Stove (see p. 90), now adopted by the military authorities. These receipts answer equally as well for the navy.

Each stove will consume not more than from 12 to 15lbs. of fuel, and allowing 20 stoves to a regiment, the consumption would be 300lbs. per thousand men.

The allowance per man is, I believe, 3½lbs. each, which gives a total of 3500lbs. per thousand men.

The economy of fuel would consequently be 3200lbs. per regiment daily. Coal will burn with the same advantage.

Salt beef, pork, Irish stew, stewed beef, tea, coffee, cocoa, &c., can be prepared in these stoves, and with the same economy.

They can also be fitted with an apparatus for baking, roasting, and steaming.

SOYER'S RECEIPT TO COOK SALT MEAT FOR FIFTY MEN.

Headquarters, Crimea, 12th May, 1856.

1. Put 50lbs. of meat in the boiler.
2. Fill with water, and let soak all night.

3. Next morning wash the meat well.

4. Fill with fresh water, and boil gently three hours, and serve.

Skim off the fat, which, when cold, is an excellent substitute for butter.

For salt pork proceed as above, or boil half beef and half pork – the pieces of beef may be smaller than the pork, requiring a little longer time doing.

Dumplings (see below) may be added to either pork or beef in proportion; and when pork is properly soaked, the liquor will make a very good soup. The large yellow peas as used by the navy, may be introduced; it is important to have them, as they are a great improvement. When properly soaked, French haricot beans and lentils may also be used to advantage. By the addition of 5 pounds of split peas, half a pound of brown sugar, 2 tablespoonfuls of pepper, 10 onions; simmer gently till in pulp, remove the fat and serve; broken biscuit may be introduced. This will make an excellent mess.

HOW TO SOAK AND PLAIN-BOIL THE RATIONS OF SALT BEEF AND PORK, ON LAND OR AT SEA.

To each pound of meat allow about a pint of water. Do not have the pieces above 3 or 4lbs. in weight. Let it soak for 7 or 8 hours, or all night if possible. Wash each piece well with your hand in order to extract as much salt as possible. It is then ready for cooking. If less time be allowed, cut the pieces smaller and proceed the same, or parboil the meat for 20 minutes in the above quantity of water, which throw off and add fresh. Meat may be soaked in sea water, but by all means boiled in fresh when possible.

I should advise, at sea, to have a perforated iron box made, large enough to contain half a ton or more of meat, which box will ascend and descend by pulleys; have also a frame made on which the box might rest when lowered overboard, the meat being placed outside the ship on a level with the water, the night before using; the water beating against the meat through the perforations will extract all the salt. Meat may be soaked in sea water, but by all means washed.

SALT PORK WITH MASHED PEAS, FOR ONE HUNDRED MEN

Put in two stoves 50lbs. of pork each, divide 24lbs. of peas in four pudding-cloths, rather loosely tied; putting to boil at the same time as your pork, let all boil gently till done, say about two hours; take out the pudding and peas, put all meat in one caldron, remove the liquor from the other pan, turning back the peas in it, add two teaspoonfuls of pepper, a pound of the fat, and with the wooden spatula smash the peas, and serve both. The addition of about half a pound of flour and two quarts of liquor, boiled ten minutes, makes a great improvement. Six sliced onions, fried and added to it, makes it very delicate.

STEWED SALT BEEF AND PORK.

For a Company of One Hundred Men, or a Regiment of One Thousand Men.

Headquarters, 12th June, 1855.

Put in a boiler, of well-soaked beef 30lbs., cut in pieces of a quarter of a pound each.

> 20lbs. of pork.
> 1½lb. of sugar.
> 8lbs. of onions, sliced,
> 25 quarts of water.
> 4lbs. of rice.

Simmer gently for three hours, skim the fat off the top, and serve.

Note. – How to soak the meat for the above mess. – Put 50lbs. of meat in each boiler, having filled them with water, and let soak all night; and prior to using it, wash it and squeeze with your hands, to extract the salt.

In case the meat is still too salt, boil it for twenty minutes, throw away the water, and put fresh to your stew.

By closely following the above receipt you will have an excellent dish.

TO COOK FOR A REGIMENT OF A THOUSAND MEN.

Headquarters, Crimea, 20th June, 1855.

Place twenty stoves in a row, in the open air or under cover.

Put 30 quarts of water in each boiler, 50lbs. of ration meat, 4 squares from a cake of dried vegetables – or, if fresh mixed vegetables are issued, 12lbs. weight – 10 small tablespoonfuls of salt, 1 ditto of pepper, light the fire, simmer gently from two hours to two hours and a half, skim the fat from the top, and serve.

It will require only four cooks per regiment, the

provision and water being carried to the kitchen by fatigue-parties; the kitchen being central, instead of the kitchen going to each company, each company sends two men to the kitchen with a pole to carry the meat.

FRENCH BEEF SOUP, OR POT-AU-FEU, CAMP FASHION, FOR THE ORDINARY CANTEEN-PAN.

Put in the canteen saucepan 6lbs. of beef, cut in two or three pieces, bones included, ¾lb. of plain mixed vegetables, as onions, carrots, turnips, celery, leeks, or such of these as can be obtained, or 3oz. of preserved, in cakes, as now given to the troops; 3 teaspoonfuls of salt, 1 ditto of pepper, 1 ditto of sugar, if handy; 8 pints of water, let it boil gently three hours, remove some of the fat, and serve.

The addition of 1½lb. of bread cut into slices or 1lb. of broken biscuits, well soaked, in the broth, will make a very nutritious soup; skimming is not required.

SEMI-FRYING, CAMP FASHION, CHOPS, STEAKS, AND ALL KINDS OF MEAT.

It is difficult to broil to perfection, it is considerably more so to cook meat of any kind in a frying-pan. Place your pan on the fire for a minute or so, wipe it very clean; when the pan is very hot, add in it either fat or butter, but the fat from salt and ration meat is preferable; the fat will immediately get very hot; then add the meat you are going to cook, turn it several times to have it equally done; season to each pound a small teaspoonful of salt, quarter that of pepper, and serve. Any sauce or maître d'hôtel butter may be added. A few fried onions in the remaining fat, with the addition of a little flour to the onion, a quarter of a pint of water, two tablespoonfuls of vinegar, a few chopped pickles or piccalilli, will be very relishing.

COFFEE A LA ZOUAVE FOR A MESS OF TEN SOLDIERS.

As I have taught many how to make it in the camp, the canteen saucepan holding 10 pints.

Put 9 pints of water into a canteen saucepan on the fire; when boiling add 7½oz. of coffee, which forms the ration, mix them well together with a spoon or a piece of wood, leave on the fire for a few minutes longer, or until just beginning to boil. Take it off and pour in 1 pint of cold water, let the whole remain for ten minutes or a little longer. The dregs of the coffee will fall to the bottom, and your coffee will be clear.

Pour it from one vessel to the other, leaving the dregs at the bottom, add your ration sugar or 2 teaspoonfuls to the pint; if any milk is to be had make 2 pints of coffee less; add that quantity of milk to your coffee, the former may be boiled previously, and serve.

This is a very good way for making coffee even in any family, especially a numerous one, using 1oz. to the quart if required stronger. For a company of eighty men use the field stove and four times the quantity of ingredients.

COFFEE, TURKISH FASHION.

When the water is just on the boil add the coffee and sugar, mix well as above, give just a boil and serve. The grouts of coffee will in a few seconds fall to the bottom of the cups. The Turks wisely leave it there, I would advise every one in camp to do the same.

COCOA FOR EIGHTY MEN.

Break eighty portions of ration cocoa in rather small pieces, put them in the boiler, with five or six pints of water, light the fire, stir the cocoa round till melted, and forming a pulp not too thick, preventing any lumps forming, add to it the remaining water, hot or cold; add the ration sugar, and when just boiling, it is ready for serving. If short of cocoa in campaigning, put about sixty rations, and when in pulp, add half a pound of flour or arrowroot.

EASY AND EXCELLENT WAY OF COOKING IN EARTHEN PANS.

A very favourite and plain dish amongst the convalescent and orderlies at Scutari was the following: –

Soyer's Baking Stewing Pan, the drawing of which I extract from my 'Shilling Cookery.' The simplicity of the process, and the economical system of cooking which may be produced in it, induced me to introduce it here.

Each pan is capable of cooking for fifteen men, and no matter how hard may be the meat, or small the cutting, or poor the quality, – while fresh it would always make an excellent dish. Proceed as follows: – Cut any part of either beef (cheek or tail), veal, mutton, or pork, in fact any hard part of the animal, in 4oz. slices; have ready for each 4 or 5 onions and 4 or 5 pounds of potatoes cut in slices; put a layer of potatoes at the bottom of the pan, then a layer of meat, season to each pound 1 teaspoonful of salt, quarter teaspoonful of pepper, and some onion you have already minced; then lay in layers of meat and potatoes alternately till full; put in 2 pints of water, lay on the lid, close the bar, lock the pot, bake two hours, and serve.

Soyer's Baking stewing pan

Remove some of the fat from the top, if too much; a few dumplings, as below, in it, will also be found excellent. By adding over each layer a little flour it makes a thick rich sauce. Half fresh meat and salt ditto will also be found excellent. The price of these pans is moderate, and they last a long time – manufacturers, Messrs. Deane and Dray.

SERIES OF SMALL RECEIPTS FOR A SQUAD, OUTPOST, OR PICKET OF MEN,

Which may be increased in proportion of companies.

Camp Receipts for the Army in the East.
(*From the Times of the 22nd January*, 1855.)

Camp Soup – Put half a pound of salt pork in a saucepan, two ounces of rice, two pints and a half of cold water, and, when boiling, let simmer another hour, stirring once or twice; break in six ounces of biscuit, let soak ten minutes; it is then ready, adding one teaspoonful of sugar, and a quarter one of pepper, if handy.

No. 16. *Beef Soup.* – Proceed as above, boil an hour longer, adding a pint more water.

Note. – Those who can obtain any of the following vegetables will find them a great improvement to the above soups: – Add four ounces of either onions, carrots, celery, turnips, leeks, greens, cabbage, or potatoes, previously well washed or peeled, or any of these mixed to make up four ounces, putting them in the pot with the meat.

I have used the green tops of leeks and the leaf of celery as well as the stem, and found that for stewing they are preferable to the white part for flavour. The meat being generally salted with rock salt, it ought to be well scraped and washed, or even soaked in water a few hours if convenient; but if the last cannot be done, and the meat is therefore too salt, which would spoil the broth, parboil it for twenty minutes in water, before using for soup, taking care to throw this water away.

No. 17. – For fresh beef proceed, as far as the cooking goes, as for salt beef, adding a teaspoonful of salt to the water.

No. 18. *Pea Soup.* – Put in your pot half a pound of salt pork, half a pint of peas, three pints of water, one teaspoonful of sugar, half one of pepper, four ounces of vegetables cut in slices, if to be had; boil gently two hours, or until the peas are tender, as some require boiling longer than others – and serve.

No. 19. *Stewed Fresh Beef and Rice.* – Put an ounce of fat in a pot, cut half a pound of meat in large dice, add a teaspoonful of salt, half one of sugar, an onion sliced; put on the fire to stew for fifteen minutes, stirring occasionally, then add two ounces of rice, a pint of water; stew gently till done, and serve. Any savoury herb will improve the flavour. Fresh pork, veal, or mutton, may be done the same way, and half a pound of potatoes used instead of the rice, and as rations are served out for three days, the whole of the provisions may be cooked at once, as it will keep for some days this time of the year, and is easily warmed up again.

N.B. For a regular canteen pan triple the quantity.

SUET DUMPLINGS.

Take half a pound of flour, half a teaspoonful of salt, a quarter teaspoonful of pepper, a quarter of a pound of chopped fat pork or beef suet, eight tablespoonfuls of water, mixed well together. It will form a thick paste, and when formed, divide it into six or eight pieces, which roll in flour, and boil with the meat for twenty minutes to half an hour. A little chopped onion or aromatic herbs will give it a flavour.

A plainer way, when Fat is not to be obtained. – Put the same quantity of flour and seasoning in a little more water, and make it softer, and divide it into sixteen pieces; boil about ten minutes. Serve round the meat.

One plain pudding may be made of the above, also peas and rice pudding thus: – One pound of peas well tied in a cloth, or rice ditto with the beef. It will form a good pudding. The following ingredients may be added: a little salt, sugar, pepper, chopped onions, aromatic herbs, and two ounces of chopped fat will make these puddings palatable and delicate.

SOYER'S SCUTARI TEAPOT.

This teapot, which is registered, is manufactured by Messrs. Deane and Dray, London Bridge, and sold by all ironmongers in the kingdom.

The top of the minaret forms the lid, and the tube which holds the tea, being moveable, allows every facility for cleaning, and amongst its many advantages the most prominent are its cheapness, elegance, and simplicity. It can be made any size.

Bill of Fare for London Suppers

In introducing the subjoined Bill of Fare, applicable to the London suppers, I must here repeat that which I have previously mentioned, that my idea is far from replacing the dishes now so much in vogue both at the 'Albion,' Simpson's in the Strand, Evans' Cider Cellars, and such-like places; but now and then a couple of dishes taken from these receipts cannot fail to prove agreeable to the partakers, without much interfering with the regular routine of the nightly business of such establishments.

PLAIN MUTTON CHOPS AND RUMP STEAKS.

Though almost anybody can boast of being able to cook a plain steak or a chop, very few can say they can do them to perfection. First of all, to obtain this important point, either the mutton or beef ought to be kept till properly set, according to season; secondly, the chop especially is more preferable when cut and beat, some time before cooking, so as to set the meat and prevent its shrinking; it at all times requires a sharp fire (the broiling City fires may be taken as an example, and the continual red heat of the gridiron); lay your gridiron over a sharp fire, two minutes after lay on your chop or steak, turn three or four times; when half done, season highly with salt and pepper, and when done, serve *immediately*, on a very hot dish. Ten minutes will do a steak of 1½lb., and about six minutes a chop.

RELISHING STEAK.

(Mutton, Veal, Pork, Chops and Cutlets, Fowls, Pigeons, Grilled Bones, Kidneys, &c.)

Chop fine a tablespoonful of green pickled chillies: mix with two pats of butter, a little mustard, a spoonful of grated horseradish; have a nice thick steak, spread the steak on both sides with the above, season with half a teaspoonful of salt, put on a gridiron on a sharp fire, turn three or four times; put on a hot dish with the juice of half a lemon and two teaspoonfuls of walnut ketchup, and serve. If glaze is handy, spread a little over the steak.

Mutton, lamb, veal, pork, chops and cutlets may be done the same; as well as kidneys; also grilled fowls, pigeons – the latter may be egged and bread-crumbed. Proceed the same for cooking according to size. Any of the above may be half done before rubbing in the chilli butter.

CHOPS, SEMI-PROVENÇAL, OR MARSEILLES FASHION.

When the chop is half broiled, scrape half a clove of garlic and rub over on both sides of the chop; serve with the juice of a lemon. For semi-Provençal, the clove of garlic is cut in two, and the flat part is placed at the end of a fork and rubbed on the chop.

KIDNEY TOAST.

Split the kidney in two, remove the sinews and outer skin, mince it up, and then chop fine; place in a stewpan some chopped eschalot and parsley, with a small piece of butter, and fry the same lightly; when done, add a small spoonful of Sultana Sauce, a little flour, and boil again; while boiling, mix in the chopped kidneys; add salt, pepper, and nutmeg to taste.

Spread the composition upon slices of toast slightly buttered; mask them up with bread-crumbs mixed with Parmesan cheese, place in a sharp oven for ten minutes, brown them with the salamander, and serve quite hot.

SANDWICHES FOR EVENING PARTIES.

Chop fine some cold dressed ham – say about a quarter of a pound, put it in a basin with a tablespoonful of chopped gherkins and a teaspoonful of mustard, a little pepper or cayenne; put about 6oz. of butter in a basin, and with a spoon stir quickly till it forms a kind of cream; add the ham and seasoning, mix all well; have the sandwich bread cut in thin slices. Have already cut, thinly intermixed with fat, either cold roast beef, veal, lamb, mutton, poultry, fowl, pheasant, grouse, partridge, &c., either of which lay evenly, and not too thick, on your bread; season with a little salt and pepper, cover over with another piece of bread; when your sandwich is ready, cut them in any shape you like, but rather small and tastily, and serve. You may keep them in a cold place, if not wanted, as they will keep good under cover for twelve hours. Chopped tongue may be introduced instead of ham, in thin slices.

MUTTON OR LAMB CHOPS A LA TURC.

Cut either thin, put on a dish, season with salt and pepper, mince an onion; pick out 20 leaves of parsley, add over a little oil, rub the chop in it well, let them soak in it two hours; plain broil sharply, and serve. This is an imitation of the Turkish kebab.

GAME FOR SUPPER.

In spite of the petits soupers de la Régence, in the early part of the reign of Louis XV., when the gastronomic art was nightly unfolding its luxurious delicacies before the illustrious guests of the Court of France, game, dressed in numerous shapes, forming the most succulent dishes, used to adorn the bills of fare of those nocturnal bacchanalian repasts which had almost triumphed over the daily festive board, the dinners then at Court being only a secondary consideration when compared with the suppers. For my part, I much prefer the former, which, as I have already mentioned, forms the focus of sociability; but when you are compelled to sup late, why not partake of game, which is much lighter food than solid meat, overdone kidneys, or oysters; for what can be more relishing and palatable for supper than the remains of either pheasant, grouse, partridge, &c., devilled or plain broiled, while plain roast game is also highly recommendable for such meals.

SOYER'S GROUSE AND BLACK GAME SALAD.

This dish is also very commendable and relishing. Roast a young grouse, not overdone; when cold, cut in eight pieces; put in a salad bowl enough salad for two persons, lay the pieces of grouse over with 2 or 4 hard eggs cut lengthwise; make the sauce thin, put in a basin a tablespoonful of finely-chopped shallot, 1 ditto of parsley, ditto of pounded white sugar, the yolks of 2 raw eggs, a teaspoonful of salt, quarter one of pepper, 2 tablespoonfuls of chilli vinegar, 4 of oil; mix all together with a spoon, whip half a pint of cream, which add carefully to your mixture; it will then constitute a delicious salad sauce; pour over your salad, and mix carefully. Pheasants and partridges, when properly kept, are also very good.

PLAIN SALAD, WITH ANCHOVIES.

Put your salad in a bowl, wash and shake well; wash and scrape a dozen of anchovies; bone them by splitting them up; have 2 hard eggs, chopped fine; put them over the salad; chop about 2oz. of either piccalilli, pickle, or plain gherkin. The above is for four persons; then add salad enough for that number; season with a teaspoonful of salt, a quarter that of pepper, 4 tablespoons of oil, 2 of vinegar; stir well, but lightly, and serve. Cos and cabbage lettuce are preferable. Anyone who does not object to oil, 5 tablespoonfuls may be used to 2 of the best French vinegar. For mixed salads proceed the same. Anchovies, eggs, and gherkins may be omitted, and yet will make an excellent salad.

RAREBIT A LA SOYER, WITH SHERRY OR CHAMPAGNE.

Cut half a pound of rich cheese in small dice; put in a stewpan 2 pats of butter with a teaspoonful of mixed Durham mustard, a little salt, half a teaspoonful of pepper, one wineglass of sherry or champagne; put on a slow fire, stir gently with a wooden spoon till properly melted, though not stringy, which might occur if turned too quickly; have a nice toast half an inch thick done at the last minute, pour your cheese over and serve. Leaving in a few minutes in an oven is an improvement.

SOYER'S UNIVERSAL DEVIL MIXTURE,
Which will be found applicable to all devilled food.

To devil the same, rub each piece over with the following mixture, having made a deep incision in any article of food that may be subjected to this Mephistophelean process. Put in a bowl a good tablespoonful of Durham mustard, which mix with four tablespoonfuls of chilli vinegar; add to it a tablespoonful of grated horseradish, two bruised shallots, a teaspoonful of salt, half ditto of cayenne, ditto of black pepper, and one of pounded sugar, two teaspoonfuls of chopped chillies, if handy; add the yolks of two raw eggs; take a paste-brush, and after having slightly seasoned each piece with salt, rub over each piece with the same, probing some in the incisions. First broil slowly, and then the last few minutes as near as possible to the Pandemonium fire. The yolks may be omitted.

HERRING A LA ROB ROY.

Well wash and clean a red herring, wipe it dry and place it in a pie-dish, having cut off the head, and split it in two up the back; put a gill or two of whiskey over the herring, according to size, hold it on one side of the dish, so that it is covered with the spirit, set it alight, and when the flame goes out the fish is done.

COLD ASPARAGUS SALAD, WHILE IN SEASON.

A very refreshing and delicious dish for supper. When this vegetable is in season, put in a soup plate a tablespoonful of vinegar, two of oil, quarter teaspoonful of salt, half that of pepper, mix together, a little chopped parsley may be introduced, and dip each head of cold grass as you eat them in the mixture.

SOYER'S CRIMEAN CUP A LA WYNDHAM.

Thinly peel the rind of half an orange, put it into a bowl with a tablespoonful of crushed sugar, and macerate with the ladle for a minute; then add one large wine-glass of Maraschino, half one of Cognac, half one of Curaçao. Mix well together, pour in two bottles of soda-water, and one of champagne, during which time work it up and down with the punch ladle, and it is ready.

Half a pound of Wenham Lake ice, if to be procured, is a great improvement.

SOYER'S BALAKLAVA NECTAR.

Thinly peel the rind of half a lemon, shred it fine, and put it in a punch-bowl; add 2 tablespoonfuls of crushed sugar and the juice of 2 lemons, the half of a small cucumber sliced thin with the peel on; toss it up several times, then add 2 bottles of soda-water, 2 of claret, 1 of champagne, stir well together and serve.

GREAT FOOD

THE CAMPAIGN FOR DOMESTIC HAPPINESS

Isabella Beeton

FIRMLY OF THE BELIEF THAT A HOME should
be run as an efficient military campaign, Mrs Beeton,
the doyenne of English cookery, offers timeless tips
on selecting cuts of meat, throwing a grand party
and hosting a dinner, as well as giving suggestions
on staff wages and the cost of each recipe.

With such delicious English classics as rabbit pie,
carrot soup, baked apple custard, and fresh lemonade
– as well as invalid's jelly for those days when stewed
eels may be a little too much – this is a wonderful
collection of food writing from the matriarch
of modern housekeeping.

'*Sublime . . . A Victorian gem*'
JULIAN BARNES

····· GREAT  FOOD ·····

NOTES FROM MADRAS
Colonel Wyvern

COLONEL WYVERN, stationed with the army
in Madras during the height of British imperial rule,
opened a cookery school upon his return to England
and was a passionate enthusiast for both
European and Indian cuisine.

In these vivid, common-sense and entertaining
writings, he gives advice on re-creating French classics
in the steaming heat; describes tiffin parties and cooking
while at camp; and laments the declining popularity of
curry in the Raj, providing foolproof recipes for curry
powder, tamarind chutney, korma and 'mulligatunny'
soup. With devotees including Elizabeth David,
Wyvern's unique brand of anglo-Indian cookery is
still reflected in the way we eat today.

*'His recipes are so meticulous and clear, that the
absolute beginner could follow them, yet at the same
time he has much to teach the experienced cook'*
ELIZABETH DAVID

GREAT FOOD

THE PLEASURES OF THE TABLE

Jean-Anthelme Brillat-Savarin

EPICURE AND GOURMAND Brillat-Savarin was one of the most influential food writers of all time. His 1825 book *The Physiology of Taste* defined our notions of French gastronomy, and his insistence that food be a civilizing pleasure for all has inspired the slow food movement and guided chefs worldwide.

From discourses on the erotic properties of truffles and the origins of chocolate, to a defence of gourmandism and why 'a dessert without cheese is like a pretty woman with only one eye', the delightful writings in this selection are a hymn to the art of eating well.

*'Marvellously tart and smart, and also
comfortingly, absurdly French'*

AA GILL

GREAT  FOOD

THROUGHOUT the history of civilization, food has been livelihood, status symbol, entertainment – and passion. The twenty fine food writers here, reflecting on different cuisines from across the centuries and around the globe, have influenced each other and continue to influence us today, opening the door to the wonders of every kitchen.